carol,

Hope you enjoy my story.

LIFE'S A PARTY!

Prayers work!

Eric "Radio" Redmon
ER

LIFE'S A PARTY!

HOW MY LIFE CHANGED IN THE BLINK OF AN EYE

Eric Redmon
with Jarvis

MOUNTAIN ARBOR
PRESS

MOUNTAIN ARBOR
PRESS

Alpharetta, GA

The author has tried to recreate events, locations, and conversations from his/her memories of them. In some instances, in order to maintain their anonymity, the author has changed the names of individuals and places. He may also have changed some identifying characteristics and details such as physical attributes, occupations, and places of residence.

ISBN: 978-1-63183-177-5

Library of Congress Control Number: 2017954795

10 9 8 7 6 5 4 3 2   1 1 2 0 1 7

Printed in the United States of America

⊗This paper meets the requirements of ANSI/NISO Z39.48-1992 (Permanence of Paper)

Scripture quotations marked "BSB" are from The Holy Bible, Berean Study Bible, copyright © 2016 by Bible Hub. Used by Permission. All Rights Reserved Worldwide. Scripture quotations marked "ESV" are from the ESV® Bible (The Holy Bible, English Standard Version®), copyright © 2001 by Crossway, a publishing ministry of Good News Publishers. Used by permission. All rights reserved. Scripture quotations marked "ISV" are taken from the Holy Bible: International Standard Version®. Copyright © 1996–forever by The ISV Foundation. ALL RIGHTS RESERVED INTERNATIONALLY. Used by permission. Scripture quotations marked "NIV" are taken from the Holy Bible, New International Version®, NIV®. Copyright © 1973, 1978, 1984 by Biblica, Inc.™. Used by permission of Zondervan. All rights reserved worldwide.

DEDICATION

To my prayer warriors:
You prayed. He answered. Prayers work!
—E. R.

To Jaxson, Jaycie, and Charlee Faith:
I hope you are as inspired by Radio as I have been.
—G. J.

CONTENTS

FOREWORD

For thirty-two years as a college football coach, I worked directly with young people. I learned how fragile these big, strong college athletes actually were when it came to dealing with traumatic life experiences. As the head coach, I could only offer limited support. I discovered that for the athlete's most complete healing and recovery, he needed the support of family, friends, teammates, coaches . . . and God. This is why I recommend Eric Redmon's book, *Life's a Party!*

After a tragic car accident, Eric faced a tremendous uphill battle from his injuries, including a traumatic brain injury. This book describes his journey with the help of his family, friends, and community. After a near-death experience, his relationship with God was renewed and strengthened. Young people today need to know that there is a way to overcome the many difficult situations that will occur during the fragile part of their teenage and young-adult lives. Eric wants to share how he accomplished his miraculous and successful recovery.

I would highly recommend Eric's book to any young person or parent who is facing a difficult time in their life.

—*Tommy Bowden*
Former Clemson Head Football Coach

INTRODUCTION

Let no one despise your youth, but be an
example to the believers in word, in conduct, in
love, in spirit, in faith, in purity.
—1 Timothy 4:12 (NIV)

When the movie *Radio* was released in 2003, it caused some confusion for many of us in Commerce, Georgia. Unfamiliar with the story the movie portrayed about a young man in South Carolina called "Radio," we were trying to figure out why a movie had been made about *our* Radio. Eric Redmon from Commerce was tagged "Radio" in elementary school. He never turned off, his mouth ran most of the time, and he had become "Radio" to everyone. His inability to be quiet often annoyed his parents, his sister Erin, teachers, preachers, and everyone else. I learned about this firsthand when I was hired to teach at Commerce High School in the fall of 1993.

To understand Radio, you have to understand his roots and where he comes from. It does not take long to figure out how important family is to all the Redmons. Radio's parents are total opposites, but they are strong influences on him. His dad, Bobby, works in construction and for the local fire department. Bobby is not loud or outspoken, but he has a dry wit and a philosophical view of life typical of Southern gentlemen. Angie, Radio's mom, is quick to point out anything that appears wrong and is willing to fight for what she believes is right. She is fiercely loyal and expects loyalty from those close to her. Nothing brings out her ferocity more than defending and protecting her children. When Radio's sister Erin was in middle school, Angie led the fight to form a competitive cheerleading team at Commerce High School. By the time Erin was a freshman, they had a top-notch team.

Besides his parents and sister, nothing means as much to Radio as his hometown, Commerce, Georgia. To Radio, Commerce is not just a town, but rather a living, breathing part of him. Whether he listens to Kenny Chesney's "Back Where I Come From" or John Mellencamp's "Small Town," Radio will tell you he feels the spirit of Commerce everywhere he goes. When you talk to Radio for just a few minutes, you realize just how much he loves Commerce. It was not until June 12, 2003, however, that Radio learned how much Commerce loves him.

I began coaching football in Commerce in 1995. The football tradition in Commerce is second to none. Straight out of John Grisham's *Bleachers*, Commerce football is known throughout the state. The Tigers won state championships in 1981 and 2000 even though they are one of the smallest schools in their classification. The team rarely has more than forty varsity players, but it is the dream of most boys in Commerce to "run down the hill" into the stadium on a Friday night. As a former coach, I can admit that one of the most exciting moments of my career was running down the hill for the state championship game against Buford in 2000. One of the ball boys for that game was eighth grader Eric "Radio" Redmon.

Radio had been a football manager for a couple of years, and I had gotten attached to him. He was the perfect combination of his parents with his dad's dry wit and sense of humor and his mother's confidence and determination. As a seventh and eighth grader, he played on the middle school football team. As assistant coach with the middle school, I was around Radio a lot. Jimbo Stephenson, the middle school head coach, and I also took care of the varsity managers and ball boys. I soon discovered that Radio and I shared a common love of history. I looked forward to the day that I would have him in my history classes.

Ironically, I actually got to know his older sister, Erin, first. Like her mom, she is a very intelligent, opinionated, and outspoken young lady as well as a very talented cheerleader. After cheering at Clemson while earning an undergraduate degree, she graduated from the University of Georgia School of Law. She was, and remains, one of the most intelligent and confident young women I have ever encountered.

When I finally had Radio in class as a tenth grader in a world history course, he did well. Since he liked US history more than world history, he was always bringing up its topics. I had to spend time every day telling him that he would have to wait until next year to discuss his topic of the day. It was usually the American Civil War that he wanted to discuss, but it was difficult to work that into the Protestant Reformation or the Renaissance. Another interest that we shared was the mystery surrounding the assassination of President John F. Kennedy. We both anticipated that discussion the following year.

While he was not the academic achiever his sister was, Radio saw things from a different point of view—and it was usually humorous. One day he came into class and completed about ten jumping jacks. When I asked him what he was doing, he said, "Since we are having a test today, I need to do something to get my brain working."

Annoyed, I replied, "Radio, your brain will take more than a *few* jumping jacks, so you need to start jumping again. I will tell you when to quit."

A few minutes later he was about worn out. I let him stop after telling him, "Now you should be really ready for the test." I really wish I could remember how he did on that test.

One of my fondest athletic memories of Radio came in the final JV game of his sophomore season. To everyone's surprise, he returned a kickoff for a touchdown against Buford, a football power and big rival of Commerce. It was a nice return and rather impressive, even though it looked to me like he was running for his life.

He was also developing into a pretty good wrestler and a better-than-average golfer. He was "coming into his own," as they say, and devoting the summer of 2003 to football workouts. On June 12, however, that all changed in a second.

To this day I don't know how I missed seeing it. I was travelling with my friend, Keith Lance, to help paint his brother's house. As we came around a sharp curve on Georgia Highway 326, I mentioned that this was where Vonte had lost control and had an accident. Vonte Reed was a student who had lived with me for a while. His car had flipped over on that curve, crushing the top, but miraculously, Vonte escaped without injury. What I did not know was that Radio had just had an accident in the same spot and was lying unconscious in the woods.

About thirty minutes later we received a phone call from Keith's daughter, Lauren. She and her mother,

Janda, were behind us, but had not arrived to help us paint. As soon as I answered the phone, I could tell something was wrong. Lauren said that there had been an accident—and the paramedics had said it was Radio.

I felt sick and I know I turned white. Someone else had already stopped and called 911. The paramedics were trying to get him out of the woods. I went back to painting with my mind racing, praying every prayer I could think of. A few minutes later Lauren called back to say that the paramedics had pulled Radio out and loaded him into an ambulance. It was going to meet the helicopter at our local hospital and fly him to Grady Memorial Hospital's trauma center in Atlanta. I will never forget her next words— "Jarvis, I think he's dead." My heart just sank.

Once Lauren and Janda arrived at the house, I left to find out more details. Summer basketball games were going on at the high school gym. I went there and found our head football coach, Steve Savage. I asked him if he had heard anything and quickly realized I was breaking the news to him. I left the gym and went by the fire station. Word had spread fast and there were over a hundred people already there, waiting to hear any news that might come. It was one of the most amazing things I had ever seen. All of these people had gathered because a sixteen-year-old kid had been in an accident. At that time, no one knew anything other than Radio was still alive and being taken by helicopter to Grady. As bad as it sounded, it was beautiful news to me. I had already figured on going to his funeral in a couple of days. Instead, there was still hope. I began praying again.

Radio spent a couple of weeks in a drug-induced coma. Grady had never seen anything like what happened in the trauma-center waiting room. Dozens of family and friends set up "Camp Commerce" for the duration. There were not just a couple of people in the waiting area, but large groups who would stay for hours. Angie and Bobby stayed with Radio throughout. Erin changed her schedule to take a lighter load at Clemson for a year and did not cheer that fall. Some people found out the Redmons were staying at a hotel close to the hospital. Wanting to help, they anonymously paid for more nights. There was still a question as to whether Radio would survive. All of us had to wait, pray, and try to hold everyone else together.

It turned out that he did survive, but he would have a long road to recovery. Ralph Waldo Emerson once said, "Life is a journey, not a destination." Radio's recovery would become the epitome of this. His journey of recovery would be long and rocky.

The most inspiring thing about Radio and his family is that they have never asked, "Why?" Radio has never openly questioned that God's will is at work in his life. He knows that this happened for a reason, and his goal is to do everything he can to reach others.

One day while we were working on school assignments, he told me he wanted to write a book because he thought his story could help others. The majority of this book is Radio telling his own story, although it includes inserts from people who have shared his journey. One of his favorite verses is Philippians 4:13: "I can do all this through Him who gives me strength." Athletes typically look at this verse and interpret it to mean that anything athletic can be accomplished through Christ. Watching Radio, I have learned that it means much more. It also means that we can endure adversity, handle success, conquer evil, and overcome temptation. Where some may see his accident as a tragedy, Radio sees it as God's mercy and part of the plan for his life.

We began working on this book in June of 2012 with the idea that it would be published on the tenth anniversary of the accident the following year. We missed that deadline and several since, but Radio is convinced that God's timing is more important than his. We also realize that there are several stories that we would not have been able to include had we met our original publication date. I mean, Radio met and asked the president of the United States a question about stem-cell research! How awesome is that?

Jackie Robinson once said, "A life is not important except in the impact it has on other lives." Radio is one of the most important people I know. I have introduced Radio many times, and I usually end by telling the audience that if his story does not touch them down deep in their souls, they need to get a spiritual checkup. My question for you is the same—are you ready for your checkup?

—*Greg Jarvis*
May 2017

CHAPTER 1

ACCIDENTS HAPPEN

*For I know the thoughts that I think toward you,
says the LORD, thoughts of peace and not of evil,
to give you a future and a hope.*
—Jeremiah 29:11 (NKJV)

Everyone who knows me calls me "Radio." I earned that nickname for one simple reason—I've always loved to talk and I don't have an off switch! I grew up in a small town and have always been happy and full of life. Then, my life changed in the blink of an eye. Like many teens, I was in a car accident, but after that the story took some unique turns. The way I was found, rescued, and "rebuilt," my near-death experience, a brief visit to Heaven, and my long road back to an active life may sound hard to believe. If I hadn't lived it, I probably wouldn't believe it, either.

Although I was just a seemingly ordinary kid, God's active intervention through family, friends, medical teams, and even strangers produced miracles for me. Even for a "doubting Thomas," these miracles and the people who helped to create them speak strongly of a loving God and His earthly assistants, or what some may call angels. My angels were ordinary people who showed up at extraordinary times. As you read, you may think of these things as happenstance or as simply "happy coincidences." After reading the whole story, you may wonder whether all these "coincidences" and their highly unlikely results were possible without God's Hand.

I've always loved being around people and having a good time, but I never considered myself particularly popular. The accident that almost took my life proved that my family and I had more friends and supporters than we ever dreamed we could have. Whether I was playing football or golf, wrestling, tagging along with Dad, hanging out at the fire department, working at Deer Trail Country Club, or going to cheerleading events with Mom and my sister Erin, I loved everything about my life as a small-town boy. You might say "life's a party" summed up my attitude . . . until June 12, 2003.

Our family history is divided into two sectors: "before the accident" and "after the accident." Mom's journal has been invaluable in informing me and reminding others about the details after the accident. I'd like to say that June 12, 2003, is a day I will never forget. To tell the truth, although I do recall the morning and afternoon hours, I don't remember much about the last part of the day my life changed forever. As a matter of fact, I don't recall much about the following couple of months, either. Most of what I know from that period has been written or told by others.

It was a typical summer day in Georgia with no hint of approaching disaster. The sky was blue, the air was hot and humid, the grass at the country club needed to be cut, and I was scheduled to the max. Right after breakfast I cut the greens on the golf courses before hustling over to the football field house for speed and agility workouts and weightlifting. I had to get in shape for football season. After a quick shower, I drove to Athens for an orthodontist appointment. No fun there.

Back home, I took a short nap before tackling the afternoon schedule.

That afternoon was as packed as the morning. First I had to substitute for my friend, Deanna Brown, who was teaching swimming lessons at my Aunt Debbie's house. Deanna had to be at Commerce High School with the other cheerleaders to paint signs for the upcoming football season. Since my sister, Erin, was a cheerleader, I knew that Deanna had to do what a cheerleader's gotta do. Growing up with a cheerleader, experience had already taught me that supporting the cheerleaders is a good thing to do. They tend to make the best goody bags. I had no idea how important the benefits of that support would be in the coming months. My plans changed abruptly when a typical Georgia afternoon thunderstorm washed out the swimming lessons. I was supposed to wait and pick up Deanna and go to a birthday party for our friend, David "Moose" Bray. With swimming lessons cancelled and nothing else to do, I called my best friend, Hank Tiller, to see if he wanted to ride with me. He was already on his way to pick up his date, and it was going to take him a while to come back to meet me. I don't remember why, but instead of waiting on Hank or Deanna I decided to go on to Moose's party alone. Looking back, I believe it must have been God's plan to keep them safe.

Between six and seven p.m., I crossed US Highway 441 on Georgia Highway 326 and headed to the party. I had driven along Highway 326 many times and was familiar with its sharp, tricky curves. I still don't know what happened or how it happened. I can't remember anything about the accident, and there were no witnesses.

Something made my Ford Explorer leave the road and flip end over end several times. The details are either gone or buried in my badly bruised brain. I have very few memories of any earthly events until three months after the accident.

***

SHANE COBB, Commerce Rescue Unit: My wife and I were eating with her sister and her husband at T-Bones, a local steakhouse, when we got the call about the accident. We left immediately for the scene and were among the first rescue workers to arrive. I knew the Redmons, so when I saw the Explorer, I was fairly certain it was Eric's. It was off the road and up in the woods, so we had to start searching for him. We started with the vehicle, and even though we didn't see him, we found enough to realize it was Eric's. We made some calls to be sure Bobby, his dad, didn't show up to work the scene as we began searching the area trying to find Eric. When we couldn't locate him, several of us lifted the vehicle to see if he was trapped underneath it. We didn't see him under it, but as we set it back down, I happened to see something white a few yards away— Eric's shirt. He had apparently crawled out of the Explorer, made his way about fifteen to twenty yards, and lost consciousness in some brush behind a tree.

Someone with a chainsaw cut a path while I let the ambulance crew know that we had to "Load and go!" meaning we had to hurry. We also called in a helicopter, but we knew we would have to meet it at the hospital. There was nowhere for it to land where we were. We got Eric out of the woods and into the ambulance and raced to meet the helicopter.

Once he was loaded and in the air, I drove back to the fire department. Over a hundred people were already gathered there to get any news they could. It was one of the most amazing things I have ever seen.

***

HANK TILLER, best friend: Radio called and asked me to ride with him, but I was already on the way to pick up my date. I told him to go on to the party and we would see him there. After picking her up, I went by his house to see if he had left. He was already gone, so we went on to Moose's party.

When we didn't see him at the party, we were wondering where he was and why he never showed up. We didn't stay too long; we had to get back to the high school gym for summer basketball camp. On our way back into Commerce, we passed the scene of an accident, but it was already cleaned up and I didn't think anything about it.

I will never forget Coach Savage pulling me aside at the gym and asking if I had heard about Radio. I was stunned as I began to realize the accident scene I had just passed was Radio's. Mom picked me up from the gym and we drove to Atlanta. I hoped and prayed the whole way that it wasn't as bad as everyone was saying.

***

The few memories I do have from the period immediately after the wreck are spotty, but also strong and powerful. At some point during the early hours after my accident, I realized I was briefly in Heaven. I remember the beauty, the streets of gold, and feeling peace. I saw and recognized my cousin, Greg, who had passed away when I was eight months old, and Papa

Martin, my mom's dad, who died in the 1990s. I didn't talk to anyone; I was just there for a short period and I didn't want to leave. When I tried to tell my parents about this, I could only say individual words, not sentences. It took several days for them to figure out what I was trying to tell them.

This experience strengthened my faith and made me want to do God's will even more than before. In her journal, Mom recorded my telling them my experience, saying that it was "real" and that I loved Jesus more than I loved them.

***

ANGIE'S JOURNAL: Eric, you keep talking about roads, Heaven, gold, Papa, and Greg. We continue to pray that we will understand you and that you can tell us more. Right now, we are just thankful you can talk.

***

My story is not about anything that happened in Heaven, though, but about everything that happened here. It is about how my faith, family, and friends came together to help me rehabilitate my body and the lessons I have learned on my incredible journey.

CHAPTER 2

BACK WHERE I COME FROM

Train up a child in the way he should go,
And when he is old he will not depart from it.
—Proverbs 22:6 (NKJV)

To understand me and my story, it helps to know a little bit about my family, and how important my hometown, Commerce, Georgia, is to me. One of the greatest blessings God ever gave me was letting me live in this place where God, country, and family still matter. Regardless of the world's rich offerings of lifestyles and places, I give thanks daily for my life here. Other than my family, this town and its people are the biggest and best influences in my life and my strongest support team. I am proud and thankful to be a part of this community that not only molded my life, but quite literally helped to save and rebuild it.

With fewer than seven thousand residents, Commerce is one of the smallest towns in Northeast Georgia, but it

has a rich history and strong traditions. This area has always been a trade center. First, it was an important Native American trading and traveling trail dating back to the Apalachee people. Early settlers established a community and trading center called Harmony Grove shortly after the American Revolution. In 1876, the Northeastern Georgia Railroad built a line from Athens through Harmony Grove to Lula (near Gainesville, Georgia), bringing more changes and additional businesses. The railroad's ownership has changed several times, and now Norfolk Southern trains run through our town, bringing and taking freight while adding their unique sounds and flavor to our lives.

When residents decided that Harmony Grove wasn't a suitable name—another town in Dawson County had the same name—they appealed to the Georgia legislature and the name was officially changed to Commerce in 1904. Like my nickname, it stuck. Although it remains a small town, there is nothing small about Commerce's influence. From athletes and authors to pastors and politicians, our residents have made their marks. Dr. L. G. Hardman was elected governor of Georgia in 1927 and served two terms. Using its old name, Harmony Grove, Olive Ann Burns made it the setting for her book, *Cold Sassy Tree*. Country music star "Whispering" Bill Anderson wrote his famous song, "City Lights," while living in the Andrew Jackson Hotel in Commerce. While some citizens have become successful professional athletes, writers, and politicians, countless others are quiet heroes, unsung and often unrecognized, but irreplaceable. Our people cling to our small-town charm and work hard to maintain it for future residents. We are proud of our history and continue to build on its solid foundation while creating new traditions and new claims to fame.

To me, there is nothing in the world like living in a small Southern town. To be honest, I feel sorry for people who can never have that experience or even know what it's like. Perhaps the best way to describe Commerce is to compare it with Mayberry on *The Andy Griffith Show*. Our people and places have different names, but many of them are quite similar to their Mayberry counterparts. For many years, Morgan Edwards owned the local barbershop (definitely not a style shop!), offering haircuts, news, and advice while providing an endless source of local information (i.e., gossip). With his fluffy white beard, Morgan makes a great Santa Claus every Christmas, too. Huck's Café is still open for business and continues serving the best burgers and BBQ in the area. Commerce Drug and Sanders Furniture have been downtown fixtures for over one hundred years. Because the railroad tracks divide the main street through town, a long-standing rite of passage for teenagers is to spend Friday nights "circling the tracks" in their cars. They will ride through town on one side, then cross the tracks and head back the other way, usually ending up at the Dairy Queen on the south end of town. There are no gangs in Commerce, just lifelong friendships and loyalties. Our local characters are as memorable as those in Mayberry.

Before my accident, I was living a typical Southern lifestyle. I was born January 20, 1987, at Northeast Georgia Hospital in Gainesville, Georgia, and spent my first few years in Maysville. My family moved to Commerce in 1991, fell in love with the town and its people, and have lived here ever since. Commerce has always felt like home to me and probably always will.

They say you can't go very far in any direction in the South without seeing a church of some kind. This description certainly applies to our area, where churches play significant roles in personal, family, business, and community affairs. Both my parents grew up just across Interstate 85 from Commerce. Although Mom was reared as a Baptist and Dad was brought up in a Holiness church, local churches helped them and their friends to develop similar strong Christian values. There is no doubt in my mind that those traditional values, which were passed on to Erin and me, as well as to our friends, have helped us to survive the trials we've faced.

My dad, Bobby, has been a construction worker and a fireman as long as I can remember. His background in those fields played a major role in my recovery after the accident. Beginning at age four, I tagged along with Dad to work sites to "help" him in the summertime. He and his buddies didn't just "put up" with me; they made me a part of the crew, finding or creating jobs for me to do. I always hated for school to start back in the fall, not because I wanted to play, but because it interfered with my "working" and cut into my time spent with Dad. I guess so much time together is why I'm so much like him when it comes to being laid back and easygoing. Dad isn't very outgoing, doesn't talk much, and has never liked people who brag or talk a lot about themselves. His lessons for me included, "Don't tell folks what you can do; show it on the field." and "Never run your mouth at an opponent." I've learned so much from Dad—except how to keep my mouth shut!—and he still shares his wisdom with me. I love our relationship because we are the best of friends.

Dad has been a member of the Commerce Fire Department for more than twenty years, and as a child, I loved hanging out with the firemen. During the school year, Dad used to pick me up from the Methodist preschool and take me to the local drugstore for lunch with Bob Nelson, one of the firemen. My adventures as an unofficial, but very active, Commerce fireman were filled with activities any boy would dream of doing. Though they never gave me the title, I think I've always been their mascot. Like mischievous guardian angels, they teased me, picked on me, played tricks on me, and aggravated me constantly when I was little, and they haven't let up on me to this day.

When I was about six years old, an alarm came in while I was riding with Dad. With no idea how serious this fire was and no readily available alternative, he just took me with him to the fire. Seeing that all hands were needed, he put me and my books in a bin on the equipment truck and ordered me to stay there until he came back. In the stress and excitement of fighting stubborn flames in a high wind, Dad and the other firemen forgot about me. When I got tired of looking at my books, I climbed out of the bin, but stayed on the truck, watching the activity and loving the excitement. Eventually they put out the fire and Chief Spear came back to the truck. Seeing me, his jaw dropped and he asked several questions without waiting for answers: "Eric Redmon, what the heck are you doing on this truck? How did you get up there anyway? Does your daddy know where you are?"

"Yes sir, Dad knows where I am. When we got here, he put me in that bin right there and told me to stay up here until he came back for me. I've been good—I didn't get down and I didn't mess up anything."

My folks still cringe when someone tells that story. I cringe at more breathtaking memories, like the time they put me in a rolling Coke cooler and rolled me down a hill behind the fire department—an unforgettable stunt!

My favorite time of year was spring, when the fire department put on its annual fundraiser, the Chicken-Q. As the event grew over the years, we would start cooking the afternoon before and stay up all night cooking thousands of chickens. My first job at Chicken-Q was spraying a salt-water solution on the chickens cooking on the grill. This kept them from drying out and burning, and kept me busy, but not quiet. As years passed, I was promoted to the most important job of all, spraying sauce on the chickens. Getting the right amount on each chicken at the right time was crucial to making the best-tasting barbecued chicken in the country. I still remember waking up to the sound of a pitiful rooster crowing as someone announced, "Rise and shine, it's Chicken-Q Time!"

Because Commerce Fire Chief J. Nolan Spear and my uncle, Sam Brown, let me and my imagination run loose in the fire department—checking out the equipment, playing on the trucks, climbing on the hoses, etc.—my boyhood goal was to become a fireman just like my heroes. Who knew they would actually be the heroes who saved my life?

Much like being a fireman, the outdoors has always been important to Dad, and he has passed that love on to me. Dad and his friends didn't send their sons away to camp during the summer—they took their sons with them to deer camp and other outdoor activities, building lifelong bonds and memories. It almost didn't happen, but I killed my first deer and acquired my nickname, "Radio," at the same deer camp when I was ten years old. In the excitement of getting ready to go hunting during doe season, I remembered my gun, but I forgot my bullets! By the time I thought about them, it was too late to go back, so I just kept quiet and didn't tell Dad about my goof. We had only been in the deer stand a few minutes the next morning when a doe walked out of the woods in front of us and just stood there like she was waiting for me to shoot. Dad whispered, "Now's your chance, Eric! Aim careful and shoot straight!"

I whispered back, "I can't. I forgot my bullets!"

Dad didn't hesitate. "Here, use my gun."

His gun was way too big for me, and it would kick like a Georgia mule! Dad used an extra hand to steady the gun, help me aim, and keep one hand positioned so the kickback wouldn't hit me in the eye. He whispered again, "Now shoot—she's not gonna wait on you all day!"

Holding my breath, I squeezed the trigger. Miraculously I killed that deer with my first shot. Dad was proud of me—and quite relieved that my eyes, face, and shoulder were still intact and unbruised. I was the happiest, proudest hunter in Georgia, if not the whole world!

That was also the year one of the guys nicknamed me "Radio" and explained it to everybody like this: "That boy is like a radio—he talks all the time! Trouble is, he ain't got an off switch." The nickname stuck like superglue.

That fall I began the fifth grade and my first year as a manager for the high school football team. Michael

Fitzpatrick, a senior fullback, had been at deer camp. He started calling me "Radio" at football practice. Fitz was one of our best players and a team leader, so it didn't take long for everyone, including some of the coaches and especially Coach Rex Gregg, to pick up on it. The next thing I knew, everybody was calling me "Radio," and that's what I've been known as ever since.

***

My mom, Angie, has always been the biggest cheerleader for me and my sister, Erin. Even though I was very close to Dad, it was easier for me to talk with her about important things. Mom stayed at home with me until I started school. Then she went to work as a project coordinator at Baker & Taylor, a wholesale book distributor in Commerce. Dad was always working at his construction job or the fire department, so she ended up being the chief chauffeur, defender, "go-fer," equipment manager, and coach for Erin and me. Unfailingly supportive in everything we did, she never missed a football game, wrestling match, one of Erin's cheerleading competitions, or any other activity involving either of us.

Looking back, there was actually one occasion when Mom didn't support me at first, but she eventually came around. When I was seven or eight, I decided to play flag football and I needed some cleats. Erin had outgrown a pair of cleats that were my size. When Mom handed them down to me, I was shocked, outraged, insulted, and definitely rebellious. In my opinion, boys did not wear girl clothes or use any girl gear! Our family discussion got so heated, I declared, "I ain't wearing no girl's cleats! I'm a human being, too!" With a little nudging from Dad, Mom got me some football cleats for a boy.

Dad has always been our faithful backer, but Mom has always been the first to come to our support and defense if she feels we are being short-changed or wronged. Mom ran the house and the family while Dad was working to get the bills paid. In addition to her job at Baker & Taylor, she did the traditional household chores, made sure our assignments were done, and saw that everything regarding school, church, and sports was under control. No matter how busy we were, Mom had our supper ready every night and we ate together as a family.

My sister, Erin, is three years older than me. We've always been close, although we have very different personalities. She's a typical type A kind of person— driven to be the best at everything, very ambitious, organized, independent, and fiercely competitive—like Mom. I'm more type B—laidback, fun-loving, methodical, and competitive without the compulsion to win big at everything every time—like Dad. Growing up, Erin and I sometimes got on each other's nerves. She wanted me to be perfect like her. Despite our differences, we always "had each other's back" in a crunch.

In third grade, Erin got involved in competitive cheerleading. She wasn't satisfied just to cheer; she had to be the very best cheerleader. Five years later when Erin was in the eighth grade, she was frustrated because there was no competitive cheerleading squad at Commerce High School. Most people thought having one was a ridiculous idea, but Erin and Mom were determined to have a great cheerleading program and a winning competitive squad. The opposition never had a chance against those two.

Mom led the effort to get the program started, and Erin led the girls to develop winning teams. They fought some tough battles, but Commerce High School quickly became a cheerleading powerhouse that won several state championships. During Erin's high school career, they placed first in the state twice and second twice. Today the Commerce competitive cheerleading program is still widely respected as one of the best in Georgia.

My friend Hank and another friend, Mitch Redmon, went to Erin's competitions with me. We said we were supporting Erin, but to tell the whole truth, as we got older, we were actually checking out the girls. Competitive cheerleaders are fun, and they look good, too! Following the fire department's example, the cheerleaders quickly adopted me as their "little brother." I had several spectacular birthday parties at cheerleading competitions because we were always on the road with them in January, and cheerleaders go all out for celebrations.

***

Probably the most important thing my parents did for me was to keep me involved in church activities. They had me in church every single Sunday morning. In addition to morals, values, and how to live a good life, they taught me about faith. I learned those important lessons well while I made wonderful friends and memories attending Mount Olive Baptist Church in Commerce with my family. I accepted Christ as my Savior on January 4, 1998, and was baptized at Mount Olive on Dad's birthday, January 18, 1998. Dad let me know how special it was to have me baptized on his birthday. I was an active, but not necessarily saintly, member of the Mount Olive Baptist Youth programs, known locally as "The MOB." Every Wednesday after football practice, my friends and I went as a group to Mount Olive for our meetings. After the accident, that church and those friends played major roles in my recovery.

Our youth pastor at Mount Olive, Kevin McCook, was a great leader who had a strong, positive impact on all of us. I especially remember our conversation when a lot of my friends were getting tattoos. The temptation was strong, but I wasn't quite comfortable with the concept. I asked Kevin what he thought about getting a tattoo—would it be okay, or a sin?

That man knew the Bible and understood teenagers! Kevin didn't tell me what to do; he let me decide for myself based on my personal beliefs. "Would you be proud to show your tattoo to Jesus, or would you be ashamed and try to hide it from Him?" he asked. In other words, was I getting a tattoo to glorify God or to be like my friends? I realized I just wanted one to fit in, and that was not the right reason, so I didn't get one.

It was at Mount Olive that my faith and my relationship with God grew strong. I can't say I was an ideal young Christian who planned to be a preacher, a missionary, or anything like that, but when tragedy struck, those seeds planted at Mount Olive produced good fruit. My faith and trust in God's will were big factors for me in my fight to live and rebuild myself.

***

Although I was never pushed to participate in sports, competition and athletics have always been important to our family. Dad played football at Banks County High School. He wasn't the biggest player on the field, but he was steady and good—a team player and a workhorse.

Mom was an enthusiastic cheerleader during her high school days. My sister, Erin, played golf and softball and participated in track and competitive cheerleading from an early age. My cousin, Michael Brown, wrestled and played football for Commerce High School and was a football player at Furman University. His brother, Gary, also wrestled and played football for Commerce. Another cousin, Keith, was a professional motocross racer. All of them had a huge influence on me.

Growing up in that atmosphere, I always loved sports. When I was little, I usually had a football uniform on while I was running around playing. I learned very early that football ranks just below God, country, and family in Commerce. The entire town would shut down on Friday nights and we'd tailgate until kickoff. That's the importance of Commerce Tiger football! The only thing better than the game itself was everybody going to the local truck stop afterward to eat and rehash the plays.

The Commerce Tigers had a long tradition of entering the stadium by running down a hill at one end of Tiger Stadium. It was always the most exciting part of the game and from the time I could walk, my dream was to run down that hill on Friday night and play for Commerce. Although Commerce High School was, and still is, one of the smallest high schools in Georgia, it has a rich tradition of football excellence. I started watching my cousin Michael play when I was two or three years old. I loved running around on the field after the games because he let me put on his helmet and pretend to be a real Tiger. Later, when Michael's younger brother, Gary, played for Commerce, he let me wear his helmet, too. Wearing those helmets made me feel sure I was a part of the Tiger team. Preparing for his own days as a coach,

Gary made me eat right, exercise, and stay in training so I would be ready to play as soon as I was eligible.

Predictably, as soon as I was old enough, I started playing flag football at the local recreation department. One dad called me "Forrest Gump" because I wouldn't stop running when I scored. I don't know why, but I would just keep going and going until the coaches yelled at me to stop. Scoring was a great feeling, and it didn't take me long to figure out how to score lots of touchdowns. We were supposed to tuck the flags into our belts. Having your flag pulled off was the equivalent of being tackled. Not realizing that it was grossly illegal, I wrapped those flags tightly around my belt so they couldn't be pulled off! This worked really well until the other teams figured out my strategy. Then they not only taught me the rules, they started checking my belt before every game.

Being an official Commerce Tiger began for me in the fifth grade as their water boy and equipment manager. I loved everything about it—being on the sidelines during the games, having a part in the action, running onto the field with a tray crammed with cups of water during timeouts . . . just being on the field with the big boys was pure joy. Every game ended with me being soaking wet and freezing cold from running with cups of water all night, but it didn't matter to me at all.

There were, however, a few painful lessons in this new dream job. Being a little too proud of both my positions and my nickname got me into trouble with the coaches, which was bad, and with Mom, which was worse. When I first started managing and got my game T-shirt, I wanted to have "Radio" put on the back. Because I gave her the idea that I had permission to do this, Mom took me to get it done. My pride in my personalized shirt ended as soon as head coach Steve Savage noticed it. I can still hear him saying, "Boy, we are a team around here, not a bunch of superstars." That quickly and sternly taught me a valuable lesson about Commerce football—the Tigers are a team, not a bunch of individuals building their own reputations! I should have known better than to put my name on it anyway, because one of my heroes is Coach Lou Holtz. He didn't allow names on the backs of Notre Dame football jerseys for the same reason. Mom was "fit to be tied" with me, for misleading her and for making it necessary to buy another shirt.

Later, my being a bit too laid back cost the team a timeout and put me in Coach Savage's doghouse. Part of my job was retrieving the kicking tee and shoe from the field after kickoffs and keeping up with them until they were needed again. In one game, the Tigers scored pretty quickly and I had no idea where that shoe and tee were. While I was scrambling to find them and get them out on the field, we had to call a timeout. The short version of this story is Coach Savage was steamed at wasting a timeout and I was in hot water. After that, nobody had to remind me again to keep up with that shoe and tee!

In sixth grade, I started playing tackle football. My first injury sent me to the hospital. During a game, "Big" Ben Wilson fell on me, hurting my shoulder and exposing my ignorance of medical terminology. Dad had told me I had a broken collarbone. When I heard the doctor telling Dad my clavicle was broken, my mind raced, but couldn't come up with any answers. What and where was a clavicle and what did it do? Whatever it was, it sounded bad! I freaked out and hollered, "Oh Lord—I broke that, too?" Dad still laughs about that one.

In seventh grade, I was playing middle school football every Thursday afternoon and had been promoted to ball boy for the varsity team on Friday nights. The good news was that I still got to run onto the field during the varsity games. The bad news was the team had started using water bottles instead of cups. Why did they wait until I was no longer a water boy? As it turned out, this began two of the most exciting football seasons in Commerce's history. The 1999 season saw the Tigers go undefeated in the regular season, but they lost the semifinal game in the Georgia Dome against one of the legendary football programs in the state, Lincoln County. They broke our winning streak and our hearts, but they didn't break our spirits. The loss fueled our determination to win it all the next year.

In my eighth-grade year, the Tigers avenged that loss to Lincoln County by beating them in the regular season and also in the semifinals at the Georgia Dome. We won the 2000 Georgia State Championship the following week against another state power and one of our biggest rivals, the Buford Wolves. I couldn't wait until the next season when I would be a real Tiger varsity player for the first time.

The key to being a successful football player in Commerce was weightlifting. I got my first dose of it in the summer of 2001. Coach Savage expected his players to be in the best possible condition so they didn't wilt in the fourth quarter. When other teams were dragging and ready to quit, the Tigers were still strong and ready to roll. This philosophy dated back to our previous head coach, Ray Lamb. Since almost every coach on the Tiger staff had either played for or coached under Coach Lamb, this was a big part of the Tiger tradition. Their weightlifting and workout regimen for the team would be a critical factor in my survival and recovery.

During my freshman and sophomore years, I played on the junior varsity team, but dressed out with the varsity and played on some varsity special teams. I loved every second of it—I was finally getting to run down the hill as a part of the varsity team! I sometimes got to play on Friday nights in games where we had a big lead. Most of my action, though, was on Thursday afternoons in the JV games. In one game during my freshman year, I broke away for a long run. With a wide-open track to a touchdown, I tried to show off by switching hands—a bad mistake. I learned a lifelong lesson as I fumbled the ball and blew the chance to score. Besides the coaches yelling at me, I could hear Mom hollering, "You won't get your hot wings for supper tonight!"

Upsetting Mom enough to make her yell at me and break a family tradition of post-game hot wings stung worse than making all my coaches mad. Redemption was absolutely required, and it came just in time. I intercepted a pass late in the fourth quarter, saved the game, and regained my post-game buffalo wings. Whew!

A highlight of my sophomore year was returning a kickoff for a touchdown in a game against Buford. This time I remembered the previous year's painfully embarrassing lesson—keep that ball tucked tight with no showing off or switching hands on the way through those goal posts! Most people were surprised that I could outrun the Wolves; I was just happy to make the TD and lock in my buffalo wings.

Around that same time, some of my closest buddies and I started a new tradition. Every Thursday night a group of football players—we called ourselves the Thursday Night Crew—would spend the night together. We also called ourselves the Fabulous Five, but we may have thought more of ourselves than others did. Besides me, it included Hank, Mitch, Caleb Jordan, and Jesse Smith. A senior would drive us to my house after practice or the JV game. Other kids would come over later and hang out with us for a while. After everyone else went home, our Thursday Night Crew would download music, play video games, and have a great time until bedtime. Sometimes we plugged a microphone into the computer and recorded ourselves singing lyrics we made up. Thankfully, none of that has survived. We made a pact that our Thursday Night Crew would be a tradition until we graduated. That pact held even when the others had to drive to hospitals in Atlanta to be with me.

***

JESSE SMITH, friend: Thursday nights at Radio's were some of the best times of my life.

MITCH REDMON, friend: When Radio got hurt, it didn't make any difference to us or change our relationship—he was still our brother. We couldn't do Thursday nights without him, so we had to go to Atlanta.

***

Football was my major sport, but not my only one. Golf and wrestling were important, too. Dad loved golf and my cousins, Michael and Gary, were high school wrestlers. I wanted to be like all three of them, so those two sports were big parts of my life.

I started playing golf with Dad as soon as I could walk and loved it from the beginning. Making the high school golf team was a predictable result of all those hours on the course with Dad. We played at the local Deer Trail Country Club, which became an increasingly important place for me as the years passed. I loved hanging out there during the summer whether I was swimming, playing golf, or eating Snickers Ice Cream Bars and checking out the girls. I spent so much time at Deer Trail that I was hired to work there during my freshman year. Their golf pro, Gerald Spear, and I really hit it off. Gerald was Fire Chief J. Nolan's brother. Within a year or so they allowed me to cut the greens—one of the most important jobs there.

In first grade, I began wrestling with the USA Wrestling program. At the time, we didn't have a youth program and very few kids participated in wrestling as a sport, but I stuck with it. Commerce didn't even have a middle school wrestling program until Michael finished college and came back as a coach.

In his high school days, Michael wrestled on a state championship team. With his help, Gary became very good, too—younger brothers and little cousins have to keep up with the big guys! Once Michael was through earning his degree and playing football at Furman, he came back to Commerce High School to coach football and wrestling. Having my cousin and hero as my coach was a dream come true.

A good eighth-grade year as a wrestler was followed by a decent freshman year, even though I wasn't a younger version of my coach. I learned quickly that I couldn't "shoot" for a takedown like Michael. Like other young wrestlers, I had to develop my own style based on my strengths rather than his. My high school coach, Joe Hames, challenged me even more. He would ask me, "Are you going to be a snail or a snake, slow or quick?" As a sophomore, I was physically and technically stronger, settling into an effective style, and putting on weight. At 145 pounds, I finished in fifth place at the state tournament. My chances to improve the following year and win some major tournaments were looking good!

My diet and summer workouts going into my junior year were the toughest I had ever put myself through. I was determined to get myself into the best possible shape to have my best athletic season ever. With Erin at Clemson, maintaining and building the Redmon family's athletic image was up to me. My goal was to do that on the golf course, the wrestling mat, and the football field.

My diet was designed to put on weight and maximize the effectiveness of my workout schedule. Breakfast was three eggs, grits, and toast washed down with water and milk. At midmorning I ate crackers and a small can of tuna. Lunch was two ham-and-cheese sandwiches with chips and another glass of water. My midafternoon snack was more tuna with crackers and milk. For supper I packed down two chicken breasts with a baked potato, salad, and water. Finally, before going to bed I drank a milkshake. Adding pounds and muscle along with conditioning could open the doors to greater athletic success. To me, academics were important, but sports were even more so.

My weekly workout schedule was definitely not for wimps. I was pushing myself much harder than anybody else would have. Every Monday, Wednesday, and Friday my schedule included running, two hundred push-ups, two hundred sit-ups, and two hundred pull-ups. On Tuesdays and Thursdays, I did weightlifting and agility training at the football field house with my teammates.

Athletically, academically, and socially, I was "coming into my own" as we say in the South. I was getting stronger, heavier, and more coordinated. My grades were decent, although not as good as Erin's— staying eligible for sports was my prime motivator. Getting along with almost everyone, genuinely caring about other people, and loving to make people laugh built my popularity. My little-boy dreams were coming true! I was on track to become a major part of the football, golf, and wrestling programs at Commerce High School. Who could've guessed that God had another track and some very different plans for me? Ironically, or more likely through God's guidance, the regimen I adopted to prepare for sports prepared me for the toughest challenges of my life. Instead of facing high school rivals, I would "go to the mat" and "take the field" against death and disability in a fierce contest to live and to function as a normal person.

CHAPTER 3

CAMP COMMERCE

Two are better than one, because they have a good reward for their labor: For if they fall, one will lift up his companion. But woe to him who is alone when he falls, for he has no one to help him up.
—Ecclesiastes 4:9–10 (NKJV)

To avoid confusion, most of this part of my story is written from my perspective, although many of the memories are not mine. I can recall very little of what happened both on the way to Moose's party on June 12 and the two months following. Others shared their memories and Mom shared her journal to help me piece it together.

In the late afternoon of June 12, Taffy Carruth, a young lady from Banks County, had left her house and was driving toward Commerce when she noticed a tiny bit of smoke in the woods. Driving alone, I had run off the road, crashing through heavy brush and trees. There were no witnesses to my accident. The Explorer was totaled and partially hidden, but its engine was still running, making the rear tires spin and rub against carpet tiles that I used as floor mats. I don't know how the tiles got there, but the resulting friction caused just enough smoke to catch Taffy's attention. She made a U-turn, stopped, and called 911, starting the long battle to save my life. I still consider Taffy to be my angel, sent by God to make sure I survived. Shortly after, others began to stop as well.

***

TAFFY CARRUTH, the first person to notice the accident: It was my mom's birthday. I was at home from college for the summer and had just turned twenty years old the day before. Because my mom and I had gotten into an argument about something, I had stormed out of the house and into my car, sped up the dirt road, and made a left onto Highway 326. I was going around a curve just past the Jackson County line when I happened to look up at the sky and notice smoke coming from the tops of the trees. I said to myself, "This doesn't look right," and began slowing down a little to get a better look at where the smoke was coming from. I couldn't see clearly, but I could make out something white that appeared to be a vehicle in the woods. I stopped, got out to get a better look, and went into the woods just a little bit. I didn't want to get too close because I was scared of what might be in the woods. I could see that it was indeed a vehicle, some sort of SUV, but I couldn't tell the make or model because it was wrecked so badly. I looked into the SUV, but didn't see anyone. I tried to get closer, but couldn't because of the brush and trees. Although I wasn't able to get a good view, I could hear the SUV's engine still running and country music coming from the radio.

Walking back to my car, I reported a wrecked vehicle in the woods beside Highway 326. The ambulance and firetrucks responded quickly, but it seemed like three to five minutes before the paramedics came out of the brush carrying a handsome young man on a stretcher. I remember looking at him and thinking, "He's so cute. God, please don't let him be dead."

His eyes were open, but he was foaming at the mouth and just lying there looking lifeless. One of the paramedics said, "This is Eric Redmon, Angie's boy."

I stood there while the paramedics loaded him up in the ambulance and sped away before I drove back home crying. I apologized to Mom for acting the way that I did earlier and told her what I had seen and how I didn't think the boy was going to make it. Mom immediately said a prayer for the guy in the accident and his family.

***

LAUREN LANCE JARVIS, family friend and witness: My mom and I were on the way to help Uncle Jeff paint his house. We saw a car pulled off on the side of the road and asked the girl standing there if she needed help. She said that she had seen smoke in the woods and had already called 911. The odd thing is that neither of us saw any smoke, and I'm not sure how she saw it. It was a miracle that she noticed it at all. We waited with her until the fire department and rescue unit from Commerce got there. They found the empty car and, a few minutes later, found the driver in some bushes. It wasn't until they cleared a path and the rescue unit pulled Radio out on a stretcher that I knew who the driver was. When I saw him, my first thought was that he was already dead. He was pale, he wasn't moving, and he had foam coming out of his mouth.

***

The first emergency personnel to arrive were my friends from the Commerce Fire and Rescue units. The Explorer had flipped end over end several times, and was wedged in the trees and brush. The guys found it fairly quickly, but didn't see a driver. Shane Cobb thought he recognized the car, but wasn't sure. They immediately began looking around for a driver and any other possible occupants.

Although the Explorer was empty, the seat belt was unbuckled. Obviously whoever had been in there would be badly hurt. Not seeing anybody, they set up a search grid. After Shane spotted what turned out to be my shirt and somebody saw one of my shoes by itself not far away, they narrowed their search and found me unconscious under heavy brush behind a tree several yards from the car.

A bad seat-belt bruise on my shoulder indicated I had been buckled up during the crash. How did I get out of the car and into the bushes? I must have unbuckled the seat belt and tried to crawl to the road for help. Unfortunately, I hadn't made it very far before losing consciousness.

Just getting to me through those bushes and briars was tough even for strong men. Carrying an agitated 145-pound patient with severe and undetermined injuries out of such thick brush in rough terrain presented major problems for the rescue team. A local resident passing the scene gave them a big boost. He stopped to see what was going on, offered to help, and happened to have a chainsaw in his truck. While the EMTs worked desperately to stabilize me, this good Samaritan and the firemen cleared a path for the rescue team's stretcher.

Were all these things simply coincidences, or was there something else going on? I truly believe the Hand of God was on me and my rescuers that day.

Reports from the scene indicated I was semiconscious, agitated, and combative. All of this meant I was responding to pain and had some feeling in my body. My injuries were obviously much more severe than our small hospital in Commerce was prepared to handle. Once they had me on the stretcher and strapped down, I quit moving. Lauren wasn't the only one who thought I was either dead or dying, but our friends at the rescue and fire department threw everything they had into their fight to save me. They knew the odds were against us, but quitting wasn't an option.

Recognizing the need for quick, highly skilled help, the EMTs called in a medical evacuation helicopter to fly me to Grady Memorial Hospital's Trauma Center in Atlanta. This was Georgia's leading trauma center and probably the only place in the area equipped to handle my internal injuries. Because it was getting dark, the EMTs transported me by ambulance to our hospital and its helipad to meet the chopper. The helipad presented less risk for the helicopter crew and me than attempting a night landing and takeoff "in the rough."

Even though things weren't looking good, Commerce teams don't give up or slow down in a fourth-quarter crunch. The ambulance crew continued working desperately to stabilize me until they met the helicopter, which was waiting at the hospital when we arrived. The only thing I remember about all this is the sound of the helicopter and being scared as it was taking off. To this day, hearing a helicopter bothers me.

Grady's trauma center had been alerted when we left Commerce. As soon as I arrived, the trauma center staff began all sorts of tests, including x-rays and a CT scan. Driven by Uncle Tommy and Johnny Eubanks, my parents and Erin soon arrived from Commerce. Before they even saw me, they had to sign a bunch of permission forms for emergency exploratory surgery and other procedures. The results were a parent's nightmare. The worst things they found were swelling in my brain, a fracture of my C4 (neck) vertebrae, a collapsed lung, and hemorrhaging in my chest from a ruptured spleen. Major miracles would be required for me just to live, not to mention recover from all those injuries ranging from brain trauma to scratches. I was fighting to survive, the doctors were fighting to save me, and my family and friends were prayer warriors all night.

The trauma team removed my spleen, placed an intracranial pressure monitor (ICP) in my skull to measure the pressure created by the swelling, and did a bunch of other emergency procedures. The awful extent of my injuries really hit Mom and Dad as they heard the prognosis. If I managed to survive the next seventy-two hours, it would be minute by minute, hour by hour. Permanent, irreversible damages like being paralyzed or in a permanent vegetative state were strong possibilities.

**

ANGIE REDMON, mother: A quick shopping trip to a mall in Duluth ended with terrifying phone calls and the beginning of our family's long nightmare. Erin and I had left our phones in the car. Getting in the car, Erin noticed a missed call from my brother. When she called Tommy back, the shock and disbelief on her face let me know something was terribly wrong. I remember her telling me that Eric had been in a wreck, and they were taking him to the hospital. Erin returned another missed call from our neighbor, Lynnly Drinkard, and gave me a similar message, adding that someone was coming to Duluth to get us. That didn't make sense. Thinking he was being taken to our local hospital, I said we could drive ourselves back to Commerce. That's when Lynnly told her that Eric was being airlifted to Grady Hospital in Atlanta. Knowing that Grady had one of the best burn units around, my first thought was, "He must be burned." It never occurred to me that he was traumatically injured and possibly dead.

I had no idea our whole ordeal would be filled with examples of the ways God works in our lives. That awareness began developing immediately. We had had dinner the night before with old friends. Although they lived near the mall, we hadn't seen them in years. Now, I noticed their phone number in my car's console and called them. They came immediately, so they and Tommy arrived at about the same time. Erin and I got into Tommy's car and took off for Grady. As Tommy sped down I-85 toward Atlanta, I remember praying for Eric and thinking, **He might be flying above us at this very moment.**

After we left my friends began taking care of details for us. They picked up our car, took it to their house for safekeeping, and then headed for Grady. They kept our car for a couple of weeks, spent a lot of time with us at Grady, and set up Eric's first website so friends could keep up with him around the clock (this was before Facebook or Twitter).

God also looked out for my husband, Bobby. He was helping a neighbor work on his cabin, which didn't have phone service. Bobby usually carried his pager, but on this day nobody knew he didn't have it with him. Worried that he would hear the emergency call and show up to work the wreck, the fire department scrambled to locate Bobby while the EMTs took care of Eric. Johnny Eubanks, the acting fire chief, found Bobby at the work site, told him about Eric's accident, and drove him to Grady. When we passed them on the interstate, Bobby called us and told us to drop back and follow them. The traffic made Tommy miss a turn and lose them. We had to drive around the hospital to find Bobby, but we went in together.

The doctors met us and told us what they knew about Eric's condition, which included internal bleeding, swelling in his brain, and other scary stuff. They needed for us to sign multiple stacks of papers giving them permission to treat him, do tests, perform exploratory surgery, and put in an intracranial pressure monitor to measure the swelling in his brain. They said we could see Eric for just a minute while they were getting ready.

Erin and I had no idea what we were facing, but Bobby had seen this type of injury before. With tears in his eyes, he stopped Erin and me before we went in and warned us that Eric's head might be swollen and look out of proportion.

His head looked okay to me, so I immediately felt better. I worried about some cuts and scrapes on Eric's knees, asking the doctors to fix those, too. Bobby recognized how bad the situation was. I remember him saying quietly after they took Eric away, "That's probably the last time we'll see him alive."

***

ERIN REDMON MOORE, sister: As we drove to the hospital, I thought Eric had already died. Uncle Tommy had picked me and Mom up in the parking lot of the mall where we had been doing a little shopping before my appointment with a private tumbling coach. Our neighbor, Lynnly Drinkard, had called my cell phone to tell us about Eric's wreck. Mom and I burst into *hysterics when we realized he was being airlifted to Grady Hospital's Trauma Center. Lynnly told us to stay put and someone would pick us up. Uncle Tommy got to us just before a friend of the family arrived. Mom climbed in the front seat of Uncle Tommy's car while I got in the back. As soon as we were in the car, they both started calling Grady, trying to get any sort of update on Eric's condition. This was maddening because no one at Grady would tell them anything. Mom was also on and off the phone with Dad the whole trip. Someone from the fire department was driving him to Atlanta. At one point we passed them on the interstate.*

After numerous frustrating calls to Grady, Mom and Uncle Tommy both started screaming and crying. They described feeling just like they did sixteen years ago when my thirteen-year-old cousin Greg died in a four-wheeler accident. When I couldn't take their screaming anymore, I started yelling at them both, "Just shut up! We don't know anything yet!"

If I hadn't been in the back seat and they hadn't been so frantic, I probably wouldn't have survived yelling at them, and certainly not ordering them to shut up. We pretty much drove in silence the rest of the way except for their nonstop phone calls. My mind was churning as I started preparing myself that Eric might already be gone. I tried to remember the last thing I had said to him, but couldn't even remember if I had spoken to him that day. This was the longest car ride to Atlanta ever. I specifically remember passing every single exit between Jimmy Carter Boulevard and the Grady exit.

Once we had finally met with the grief counselor, we learned that Eric was still alive and would be going into surgery very soon, but the surgeon would talk to us first.

I stood in the hallway with Mom and Dad while a neurosurgeon explained why he needed to insert a monitor into Eric's brain. The whole time that man talked with us, his hands were shaking like a leaf—not a reassuring sight.

Dad asked, "You have done this surgery before, right?"

Mom asked, "How old are you?"

Then they asked, "Can we see him first?"

His answers were yes, he had done this surgery before, he was old enough to do this surgery, and we could see Eric. They led us into a room occupied by about four patients on gurneys. Eric was on the far left side, but Mom and Dad immediately went to the wrong person. This would be funny if you didn't realize it showed how upset they were. A nurse led us over to Eric. He looked pretty much like he always did, except his hair was messed up, he had small scratches all over his body, and he was shaking violently (from shock, we were told). It's funny, I don't remember any tubes or anything like that, just his hair, the scratches, and the shaking. To me, he looked fine—like he was sleeping. Honestly, I felt much better about his situation, but as with everything, looks can be deceiving. This time they were very deceiving.

***

MITCH REDMON, friend: We were at the beach in Destin, Florida, when we heard about Radio's accident. We had a big group with us and we immediately sat around and prayed. After the prayer my family packed, came back to Georgia, and went to Grady that night. We felt we had to be there.

***

JESSE SMITH, friend: I was on the way to the drag strip with some friends when the call came about Eric's accident. We immediately turned around. I got back in my truck, picked up my grandmother, and we took off for Atlanta. We had a tire blow out on the way, and I changed that tire in five minutes or less. My only thought was that I was about to lose one of my best friends.

***

The following days had to be the longest three days of my family's lives. Up to this point, Mom and Dad had stayed with me through every crisis of my life. Now I was fighting for my life without them, surrounded by strangers in the trauma center's intensive care unit. My family was sweating it out in the waiting room, allowed to see me only briefly every couple of hours and hearing my condition described by strangers in scary, pessimistic, unfamiliar medical terms.

I wasn't a handsome sight. By this time drainage tubes had been inserted in my head, and I also had tubes in my stomach, my nose, my mouth, my side, and who remembers where else. I was shocking to look at. Mom found every visit in the ICU overwhelming; her sugar level would drop and she would almost pass out when she left the room.

To track my progress, relieve her stress, and keep up with all the details so she could tell me about them later, Mom kept a journal for me of the entire Grady ordeal. She also took pictures of everybody who came so that I could see the party I was missing. On Day Two of her journal she wrote, "The whole little town of Commerce is praying for you, Eric." I had always loved Commerce.

This accident showed how much Commerce loved me and my family.

News of my accident traveled fast in Commerce. This was before social media, so over a hundred people gathered at the fire department that first night, hoping to get updates on my condition. Most of them didn't think I was going to make it, but they were praying like crazy for me anyway.

Tons of family and friends began showing up at Grady right after I arrived, seriously overcrowding the waiting areas. Mom called her sister, Aunt Judy, who lives in Forest Park. She was out of town, but Uncle John was home and actually got to Grady before I did. With so many people there to support us, the hospital designated a special waiting area to accommodate them. Before long, our visitors established what they called "Camp Commerce" in "their" space. They shared comfort, encouragement, food, drinks, and prayers as well as stories—mostly about me—with strangers as well as each other.

Usually people go to a hospital to visit a patient and the family. These people came all the way to Atlanta to show their support even though they knew they wouldn't be allowed to see me and might not see my parents. Because I was in a drug-induced coma, only a few were allowed to visit me. Each time someone talked to me, the ICP monitor went up, showing that my brain was responding. This was a good sign, but the staff monitored it carefully to avoid overstimulating me and raising the pressure too high.

On Day Three of Mom's journal, she wrote about not knowing I had so many friends. I didn't know it, either, but the entire Redmon family will always remember their love, support, and help.

***

TAFFY CARRUTH: Stacey Rucker, my cousin Dennis's wife, called about three days later to tell me that the boy who was involved in the wreck on Highway 326 was still alive and that his family wanted to meet me. Stacey worked at Baker & Taylor with Eric's mom.

The following Sunday afternoon, Dennis, Stacey, and their son, James, took me to Grady Memorial Hospital in Atlanta to visit Eric. James, or "Rambo" as he was called, was a classmate and teammate of Eric's. I remember walking into the waiting room and seeing a whole crowd of people there to visit Eric. Besides the family members, there were a lot of his teammates and classmates.

When Stacey introduced me to Miss Angie, Eric's mother, she grabbed me and hugged me as she said, "Thank you for saving my baby!"

Of course, I said, "You're welcome."

Surprisingly, Miss Angie asked me if I wanted to see Eric and, having no idea what to expect, I said, "Yes."

Once we entered Eric's room, I went over to him and just stared. Now he didn't look at all like the cute guy on the stretcher. He was badly swollen and had all kinds of tubes and wires going in and out of his body. Eric's dad stood beside me. After asking if it was all right to touch him, I touched Eric's hand and just watched him lying there while I prayed silently for this loving family and for this young man whose life they said I had saved. I couldn't help thinking and then saying, "If only I would've come by sooner, he probably wouldn't be lying here in a coma."

Miss Angie and Erin, Eric's sister, reassured me that it was okay, and that they were grateful that I had stopped for Eric when I came by that day.

***

Finally, at 7:02 p.m. on Sunday, June 15, the seventy-two hours were up. I was still alive—unconscious, but alive! Everyone breathed a sigh of relief that I had made it through this critical first stage. The hospital staff knew I was still in deep trouble, but few others realized it. The following Monday, they removed the ICP monitor, inserted a feeding tube into my stomach, reduced the medications, and waited for me to wake up.

I didn't come around as quickly as they had hoped. My doctors ordered an MRI of my brain on June 17. More bad news: the MRI showed a damaged artery shooting blood clots into my brain. The next decision my parents had to make was scary. A blood thinner would dissolve the clots, but it would increase the bleeding, possibly causing accidental hemorrhaging. One doctor wanted to risk using a blood thinner before the clots created further damage in my brain or elsewhere. Other doctors thought the likelihood of a severe hemorrhage was too dangerous and I might bleed to death. If they didn't use the blood thinner, the clots could break into other parts of my brain and eventually cause my organs to shut down. Either way, Dad felt whatever decision he made would kill me and he didn't know what to do. If the doctors couldn't agree on what to do, who would decide? Something had to be done quickly!

Mom was so upset that she left the meeting with the doctors. Dad's faith and common sense took charge. He asked the doctors to do two things: run a second MRI, and get my trauma team together. Then Mom, Dad, and

Erin began their own emergency healing procedures. They went into another room, started prayer chains for me in Commerce and Atlanta, got down on their knees, prayed for me, and gave me and my condition over to God. Since this was my lowest point, I believe this must be the time when I was in Heaven. If anyone noticed when I left my body, they didn't tell my folks, because there is no record of my near death or temporary death experience. That doesn't change what I experienced, though.

As Dad had requested, they ran a second MRI. After getting the results, the puzzled doctors talked with my parents. The clots were gone! Those doctors admitted they had no medical explanation as to why or how the situation had been successfully resolved. Mom and Dad knew the answer. They had given me and the problem to God, and He had dealt with those clots in His own way. From that point on my parents knew that I was going to survive. The Great Physician showed up and showed out! When the doctor told my parents that the clots were gone, Dad asked what they needed to do next. The doctor said for them to keep doing what they had been doing because it was working.

***

BOBBY REDMON, father: I don't remember a lot from Grady except our world was turned upside down and I couldn't fix it. The doctors at Grady asked us to make a lot of tough decisions. God must have helped us make them, because we certainly didn't know what to do. What I remember very clearly is that God, Grady, and prayers saved Eric's life. For that we are truly thankful.

***

ERIN REDMON MOORE: The first forty-eight hours at Grady were a blur. I remember tons of people, lots of tears, hushed conversations, and very little sleep. Eric came out of surgery in the wee hours of the next day, and they finally let us go back to see him. He was in a large room with several other people in critical condition who were being closely monitored. A nurse sat at the foot of Eric's bed. I thought he looked pretty good, especially since his terrible shaking had stopped.

I don't remember how long Eric stayed there before he was moved to a room in ICU, but I do remember clearly the night we almost lost him again. They told us at first that if he made it through the first seventy-two hours, he would be "out of the woods," so to speak. When he made it through that first critical period, we almost felt like we were home free. Then they found another problem with Eric's brain. They wanted Dad to sign a permission form allowing them to do a corrective procedure. Dad kept telling them he felt like he was signing over Eric's life, and he just couldn't do it. Finally, Dad asked them to run one more test. While they were doing that we went to the chapel to pray. When they did the test, it showed that Eric was better and the procedure wasn't necessary. Thank God!

I have a very weird memory of that time, too—the first time I felt hungry. Several days had passed before I finally asked for something to eat. At least ten people jumped up to help me choose from the spread of food and snacks our friends and family had brought into that small waiting room. They had truly "set up home for us" at Grady in the small-town tradition of staying with us and bringing tons of food for comfort and nourishment in a crisis.

That waiting room was like a constantly revolving door with families of other patients coming and going. Some of them had very sad stories. None of them "camped out" like we did or had nearly as many people there, yet we all shared whatever hope and comfort we could muster. Our group prayed with other families often, and the pastors who came to visit us would minister to them as well. One lady who also had a desperately injured teenaged son was unforgettable. Like Eric, her son had been in a wreck, so we quickly established a deep bond. She left the hospital the day her son died, but came back later that night to give us the key to a hotel room. She had paid for it so we could get some rest. Then she told Mom, "Now you go get a good night's sleep. I know Radio is going to be okay."

Two things stand out to me from this period: (1) The people—so much support from so many people. It was unfathomable. (2) The Coke billboard and the Corey Tower across the interstate from Eric's room. Rain or shine, day and night, for seemingly endless hours I stared out the window at them. The thoughts and emotions of those hours at Grady still overwhelm me every time I pass them on the interstate or see them in the Atlanta landscape. I look from the Coke billboard and the Corey Tower over to the windows of Grady, pray for the current patients and families, and thank God for His mercy to us.

***

HANK TILLER: Once I got to the hospital, it was hard realizing how bad it really was and knowing that we could have been riding in that car together. I remember thinking how things could've been different if

I would've been with Radio and just delayed him leaving the house by a couple of minutes.

***

Now the prognosis was that I would survive, but there would be brain damage—how much damage couldn't be determined until I woke up. Along with renewed hope for my survival came steps to recover and rebuild my strength. Since eating was out of the question, they started a high-protein diet through a feeding tube in my stomach. Now it was up to me and God to rehabilitate my body, mind, and spirit.

On Day Six, Mom wrote that I finally opened my eyes and squeezed her hand. Then, I squeezed Erin's hand very hard, and that gave everyone hope that I was really going to make it. I was still in a coma, but I was showing signs of life. Many of my friends and family were still hanging out in "their" waiting room. Others were calling a phone in the waiting area to get updates. I found out later that they were worried sick, but in good old Southern fashion, they found strength and comfort by creating an almost party-like atmosphere in the waiting area. My incredible "Commerce Cheerleading and Support Team" shared snacks, food, drinks, prayers, and stories—mostly about me—as I fought the hardest game of my life. I'm sure that Grady Memorial Hospital had never seen anything like this. Knowing that I would hate missing my own party, Mom took pictures to go with her journal so I could relive it later when I finally woke up from the coma. With my family, it was always "when, not if," I woke up.

***

GREG JARVIS, Eric's teacher and coach: I will never forget going into the waiting area and seeing all the people who were there. There had to be at least fifty—hanging around, eating snacks, and telling stories about Radio. It was the most unusual thing I had ever seen, but somehow it seemed appropriate. His aunts were there and Erin came out to give us updates.

When Angie learned I was at the hospital, she took me to see Radio. As a teacher and coach I have visited many students in the hospital, but I was not prepared for this. Eric looked terrible and had tubes coming out of the top of his head, out of his stomach, just everywhere. The only good news was that he was breathing.

I hated it so much for Radio and his family, but their faith and strength to deal with their son's disaster absolutely amazed me. We had all come together to support the Redmons, yet their faith and strength provided strength and inspiration for everyone else.

***

Mom, Erin, and either Aunt Debbie, Uncle Tommy, or someone else from Mom's family slept at the hotel every night after that while Dad stayed in the hospital with me. Commerce really displayed its generous, loving heart. People who wanted to help us went by the hotel and anonymously paid for additional nights for them. They also made certain that someone from Commerce came every single night to be with Dad so he wouldn't be alone if things went bad. Usually it was my Uncle Sam or Gary Tiller, Hank's dad, who stayed with him.

That was only the beginning. Friends brought snacks for "Camp Commerce" plus lunch and supper for my parents and Erin every day so they didn't have to leave the hospital to eat. Dad feels strongly that because we are fortunate enough to live in such a supportive community, we should always share with others. There was so much food that Mom began sharing it with other families at Grady who were going through similar situations. "Camp Commerce" also led a prayer circle every night, lifting all of us in the trauma center and our families up to God. By the time we left Grady, these friends and strangers had become like family.

Since my accident occurred several years before Facebook and Twitter, the website my Mom's friend set up was really important. Mom would post daily updates on my condition, and people could write notes of encouragement to me. It was amazing how many people we barely knew or didn't know at all began logging on, checking on me and leaving messages. Love and caring are universal. Some of these folks were from other states as far away as Hawaii; some were from other countries.

"Pray for Eric" signs began popping up all over Commerce. With every day showing some improvement in my condition, Mom developed a new slogan: "Prayers work!"

On Day Nine, because my nerves were beginning to "wake up" I was so agitated the Grady staff had to tie my hands down. This was hard for my parents, but it was actually a good sign—I could move my arms and was trying to come out of the coma. In her journal entry, Mom wrote that I looked scared, and she was scared for me. Like she has done my entire life, though, she gave it to God and let Him handle it.

On Day Eleven, the doctors turned my ventilator down to begin fighting a staph infection. Why did bad stuff have to pull another end run around my progress?

On Day Thirteen, the staff turned my ventilator down again, this time hoping to take me off it within two days. I was showing even more agitation at being restrained, but they had to keep my hands tied down so I wouldn't pull out my tubes. Even in a semiconscious state, I wanted those tubes out!

On Day Fourteen, Thursday, June 26, I was finally breathing on my own! It was pure oxygen through a tracheotomy tube, but I was breathing by myself even though I was still only semiconscious.

The following day the ventilator was removed. I was still breathing pure oxygen rather than room air, but I didn't need a ventilator to breathe for me. The doctors increased my medication so I would rest and get stronger, rather than waste my energy fighting the restraints.

It was time to plan the next phase: R & R (recovery and rehabilitation, not rest and recreation!). When Dad asked one of the doctors for advice, he got a blunt answer: "If you put Eric in a corner and do everything for him, he will just sit there and never recover. He needs stimulation and an aggressive rehabilitation program. The best thing for Eric will be the hardest for you. Treat him like you did before the accident, push him to recover, and don't let anybody 'baby' him."

My athletic conditioning was enabling my body to heal steadily. My brain, however, wasn't healing so well, and rebuilding some of my brain functions would turn out to be very difficult. Maybe I should have been more like Erin and done more studying and brain conditioning! No one could measure the full extent of my traumatic brain injury (TBI) until I was fully conscious, and that simply wasn't happening at Grady.

My parents looked at various rehabilitation centers and decided I would respond best in an environment of young patients instead of adults. The plan was to move me to Children's Healthcare at Scottish Rite on June 30.

The next step was transporting me to Scottish Rite, my home for the next three months. The accident dragged me backward from a healthy, "can-do" athlete in sweats to a sick, helpless weakling in diapers. Now I had to relearn all the basic tasks of living, including the simplest ones like eating, talking, walking, and using the toilet. It was going to be a long, hard road, but athletes are trained to never quit.

CHAPTER 4

SCOTTISH RITE

A friend loves at all times, and a
brother is born for adversity.
—Proverbs 17:17 (NAS)

The traumatic brain injury (TBI) I suffered continues to cause most of my ongoing problems. I'll explain it in football lingo because medical terms are hard to pronounce, tough to spell, and difficult to understand.

According to the medical playbook, the nervous system regulates and coordinates the body's basic functions and activities. Its major components are the central system and the peripheral system. The central nervous system with the brain and spinal cord are the coaching staff coordinating the quarterback calling plays on the field and all the specialty teams. The peripheral nervous system includes all the other players on the body's teams. It connects the central nervous system to the organs, limbs, torso, muscles, etc. and delivers signals to them.

When something bad happens to any part of the nervous system, it loses the ability to carry out its duties. The car accident made very bad things happen to many parts of my nervous system, including my brain. My accident was the equivalent of a gang tackle with unnecessary roughness and unsportsmanlike conduct. It left my mind and body like teams without coaches or quarterbacks.

The brain is like a three-member coaching staff made up of the cerebrum, brainstem, and cerebellum. The part most affected was my cerebellum. Located in the *infratentorial* (a prime example of why I don't use medical terms!) region in the back of the head and the back of the brain, it coordinates voluntary muscle movements and maintains posture, balance, and equilibrium. My accident temporarily restricted blood flow to the cerebellum and then suddenly released it. To better understand this, try to picture yourself folding a water hose while the water is running, forcibly stopping the stream of water. Releasing the hose will create a powerful rush of water. In my case, that rush of blood caused symptoms similar to a stroke.

The sides of the brain, known as the temporal lobes, are the team statisticians. They keep up with the mind and body's current activities (short-term memory) and history (long-term memory). My injuries acted like a radio's off switch, silencing signals to many parts of my body. Not having access to my memories created major difficulties in my recovery. For example, when I finally began to talk again, Mom and Dad realized that I couldn't remember anything. Not only was my memory of the accident gone, now I couldn't remember things from minute to minute, either. We would have to rewrite the scripts, rebuild the switches, and repair many parts of my brain and body. Although we didn't know it then, most things would improve over time, yet nothing but faith would ever come back to pre-accident level.

Still semiconscious, I was moved to Children's Healthcare of Atlanta at Scottish Rite on Monday, June 30, to begin my rehabilitation. Erin rode with me in the transport van while Mom and Dad followed in the car.

Mom was excited because she had finally been allowed to give me a sponge bath and brush my teeth for the first time in two weeks. Knowing Mom, my cleanliness had probably been a major concern since my accident. Being hooked up to tubes and monitors at Grady had made it impossible to have a real bath, but having me dirty definitely added to Mom's discomfort.

My room at Scottish Rite was very different from the sterile, clinical atmosphere of Grady's trauma center. The staff asked my parents to decorate my room with things from home and to make a scrapbook of pictures to stimulate my brain and memory. As usual, they went all out. With help from our friends, Mom, Dad, and Erin created "Radio's Station" at Scottish Rite with my football jersey and helmet, my bedspread from home, and a lot of South Carolina Gamecock stuff, including a signed letter from my hero, Coach Lou Holtz. My friend Hank brought a poster of the Olsen twins "for visual stimulation." Our goal had always been to move to California and each of us marry one of the twins and let them take care of us. All of this was done to bring a sense of "home" to my room and to make sure I felt comfortable and safe when I regained full consciousness.

***

ANGIE REDMON: Grady's atmosphere was mostly "gloom and doom." They gave us "worst-case" scenarios, and sometimes it seemed like they weren't sure what was going on with Eric. Scottish Rite's atmosphere was the total opposite. They immediately started telling us that they were going to put his clothes on and get him up the next day and begin rehab. I tried to tell them that they couldn't do that because he had just gotten out of the ICU. It was really amazing to see how they got him dressed and brought in a lift to get him out of the bed, but it was also an emotional roller coaster.

Now we weren't worried about his surviving, but rehabbing. I remember thinking that God had given me a new job: to help Eric get better. I went through a period when I was mad at God, didn't want this challenge, didn't feel strong enough to handle it, and just wanted my Eric back the way he used to be.

The biggest reality check was realizing that this was going to take a long time. I had thought Eric would get back to playing football in the fall, but I began to realize that wasn't going to happen. He had to relearn how to hold his head up—there was no way he was going to play football!

As a mother, I was used to "fixing" everything, and I couldn't fix this. I had to learn to turn it over to God, but this was the hardest thing I ever had to do. Looking back, it should have been the easiest thing to do. I used to pray for patience; I never realized that this would be the way to learn it.

***

For the first few days at Scottish Rite, we weren't allowed to have any visitors. Adapting to my new surroundings and allowing Mom and Dad time to deal with my situation required some privacy.

My family and friends continued to support me at Scottish Rite as they had at Grady. Dad stayed with me at night while the others slept in a hotel. When I was agitated, Dad figured I was scared—and I probably was. He would stand next to my bed, comforting and talking to me until I calmed down. As time went on, Dad could just tell me he was there and I would settle down.

July was my time to start making real progress toward recovery and regaining independence. It was a terrible reality check for Mom, Dad, and Erin. They still expected me to recover, walk out of the hospital in a few weeks, and be ready to play football in the fall. Understanding the full extent of my injuries and the enormous sacrifices they would have to make began hitting them like bone-jarring gang tackles. The numbness caused by the initial shock and fatigue wore off as these grim facts slammed into them. All three of them fought through mixed emotions as my doctors and therapists explained the whos, whats, whens, and whys of my condition and treatment plan and introduced a whole new playbook for my life and theirs.

On Tuesday, July 1, I took a step toward being a person instead of a patient. My new caregivers dressed me in real clothes instead of "bare your backside" hospital gowns.

On July 2, they lifted me out of bed and strapped me into a wheelchair for the first time. I was still only semiconscious and didn't have enough motor skills to balance myself, but I was "up"! The idea was that getting me out of bed might help rouse me to full consciousness. Continuing stimulation from dedicated therapists would go a long way toward reactivating my body and brain.

The amount of therapy I received shocked my parents. They saw my semiconscious state as making me unable to do anything for myself; my therapists saw a boy they could help get back to full consciousness and a full life. Mom and Dad were a bit nervous even though they were impressed with the aggressive approach. Rejoicing at my responses, they kept watchful eyes and positive outlooks on everything.

***

BOBBY REDMON: Scottish Rite was a different world from Grady. They were all about helping Eric get his life back and they started rehab right away. They expected 100 percent from everybody—him, their staff, and us. There were ups and downs for the next several months, but their goal and ours was always to get Eric 100 percent well.

***

When I arrived at Scottish Rite, I was at level two on the Ranchos Los Amigos brain-injury assessment scale. This meant I was conscious, but that was about it as far as my capabilities were concerned. Ranchos Los Amigos is a research and rehabilitation hospital specializing in brain trauma. They devised this eight-level scale to determine the severity of closed head injuries like mine. Higher numbers indicated more progress.

I was too mentally sluggish to process and remember many details of my rehabilitation at Scottish Rite. To prod myself, I've studied the pictures and videos, but my memory just won't bring stuff back. Mom, Dad, Erin, and others have to tell me most of what happened. I know I had to wear braces on my hands and feet to keep the muscles from contracting and locking up. They said watching me improve was like seeing a baby learn how to do things for the first time. One of Mom's lowest points came when they took out the bladder catheter and put a diaper on me. Seeing her athletic sixteen-year-old son back in diapers was almost unbearable.

Scottish Rite's therapists helped me do all kinds of exercises to loosen and build up my damaged muscles. I even had to relearn how to breathe without a tracheotomy tube and how to talk. Don't forget that everyone has called me "Radio" since my elementary school days. Being able to talk again was going to be a top priority for me!

On July 4, Mom wrote that I counted to ten and said "bye" to my therapist. Even though I was only mouthing the words, this was a major improvement.

The next day, July 5, was weigh day. The scales stopped at a "whopping" 108 pounds. Now I weighed less than most cheerleaders! After all that grueling work to gain weight and strength, I had lost almost one-fourth of my body weight. Losing another ten pounds would make me an official 98-pound weakling—unacceptable! The bright side, as many doctors told my parents, was that my conditioning regimen had probably saved my life. Those strong muscles had protected my bones and internal organs.

With the imminent risk of dying out of the way, our biggest challenge was grappling with my brain injury. The only way to attack that was with more and more therapy. Once again, my training style came into play— I was used to following a tough training regimen and working hard to reach my goals. Even when recovery was still a long way off, I possessed a secret weapon: the work ethic instilled by Dad and my coaches. This made it easier to slog through all the physical and mental therapy and to keep the drive needed to recover.

The longer I stayed at Scottish Rite, the harder I worked. A big problem with my speech was not getting enough air into my lungs to push words out through my larynx. I had to improve my breathing before I could talk. The benefits of all those wind sprints and jumping jacks were lost, and now I couldn't do them to regain their benefits.

I didn't appreciate her efforts at the time, but Erin helped my speech therapy tremendously by aggravating me until I just had to yell "Stop!" We both got frustrated because barely a sound came out even when she tried her hardest to make me really mad, mad enough to breathe deeper and force out more air from my lungs so I could yell, "Stop!"

Like a good sister, she also added some pleasant touches to our efforts. Erin played some of my favorite music so I could mouth the words. Whether it was "Margaritaville" by Jimmy Buffett or Lynyrd Skynyrd's "Sweet Home Alabama," I was finally able to start putting words together and get them out so they could be heard.

On July 7, I went the entire day with my tracheotomy tube plugged. I was breathing better and my lungs were healing! We hoped they would remove the tube shortly.

The next day, July 8, I made two big accomplishments: I moved my left leg and ate some chocolate pudding, although I still had a feeding tube in my stomach. Mom was still frustrated and wrote again that it was like starting over from when I was a baby. They were excited each day to see what I could do next.

By July 11, I was making progress on several fronts, but still having problems on others. On this particular day, I ate a little oatmeal and actually sucked juice from a straw! This was a huge improvement because this was not a reflex, but following a command from my brain. On the bad side, muscle spasms in my arms were making them twist like pretzels. My doctors decided to try giving me Botox to loosen the muscles and make them relax. If it worked, they could put braces on my arms to give me better control and more range of motion. The biggest thrill of the day was my parents taking me outside to the goldfish pond! Can you imagine a sixteen-year-old athlete finding a visit to a goldfish pond exciting? Think about it—other than the ride from Grady to Scottish Rite, this was the first time I had been outside since the accident. Anything outside was more exciting than hospital walls and halls.

Removing my tracheotomy tube was the next big thing on the agenda. Unfortunately, that required passing a sleeping test. Basically, I had wires and monitors hooked to me all night, and I had to prove that I could breathe on my own throughout the night. Since I hadn't been able to do that, I had to keep my tracheotomy tube.

July 13 was another big day. My therapists helped me stand up! I mouthed "Shorty" at my friend Hank as they stood me up. Later I kissed Mom.

I know from reading her journals that Mom was praying constantly for me. She wrote many times how she missed things like our talks and the music we shared. I hated that she was hurting so much. Dad and Erin were hurting, too. Dad stayed with me every night since the accident and Erin gave up cheerleading at Clemson for the 2003 football season to help me as much as she could. Without their support, I couldn't have progressed nearly as well or as fast I did.

***

ERIN REDMON MOORE: Giving up cheerleading for a year to help Eric wasn't a hard decision for me. When something bad happens, people often play the "blame game" or the "what-if game." After Eric's accident, all of us played these painful mind games separately and together. On a rational level, we knew that we hadn't caused the accident that threatened to destroy my brother, our family, and our dreams. Still, "what-if" questions buzzed around our minds. My chief target of blame was cheerleading, because I had made it such a huge part of my and our entire family's life. Now I was finally realizing the results of all those years of hard work and big dreams. Although I had reached my goal of cheering for a major university, my excelling at cheerleading was still a primary focus for all of us. I had several tumbling sessions and a work weekend on campus for cheerleading practice scheduled the week of Eric's wreck. Since I had developed a slight mental block about some of my skills, our family was focused on removing that block. In fact, on the very night of Eric's accident, Mom was taking me to a private session with one of the best tumbling coaches in Atlanta. A sports psychologist was going to meet us there. My carefully constructed world exploded with Eric's accident; the importance and magic of cheerleading fell apart and "what-ifs" and "if onlys" invaded my thoughts.

It was a wake-up call for me. So much more mattered in our lives besides that stupid mental block and my cheerleading career. It's embarrassing to think about Eric's accident happening in the midst of all that focus on my cheerleading. After all these years, the "what-ifs" that still creep into my mind include, What if everyone in the family including Eric hadn't been so focused on my cheerleading career that week? What if Mom and I hadn't gone to see the tumbling coach that night; would Eric's plans have been different? What if I hadn't spent so much energy on cheerleading that week; would I be able to remember the last words I spoke to my brother before his accident?

In light of all this, cheerleading just lost its appeal for me. There was no way I could go back to school and cheering less than two months after Eric's wreck. Spending all my time in Clemson, oblivious to what was going on at home, was unthinkable. I did go back to school, but only for classes on Tuesdays, Wednesdays, and Thursdays. Other than that, I was at home or in Atlanta with the family, helping every way I could.

In the spring, Mom and Dad wanted me to try out again for cheerleading and had me see a counselor about my decision. In the end, I did cheer for one more year, mainly because they wanted me to, but the appeal was gone. I even wondered if God had allowed Eric's accident to happen as a wake-up call to me about my priorities. Years later, I still love cheerleading and always will, but I don't regret my decision to give it up for Eric. It just didn't matter as much anymore.

***

July 15 was the first day of football camp. I missed it, not even aware that practice had started. The team told my folks they really missed me and clapped "three times for Radio" at the end of each session. I was becoming more aware of my surroundings and eating soft foods, but for the first time since my toddler years, football wasn't even a blip on my radar. Both my arms and one foot were in braces, so my physical and occupational therapy were fairly light. One slight change in my room made a big difference, though. Mom noticed me watching television, so she moved my bed to make me turn my head more and focus on the screen. My eyes were slanted down, and this forced me to move them up toward the television.

On July 16, I finally slept through the night and passed the sleep test! Now another pesky tube could go away.

They took out the tracheotomy tube on July 17. My throat was sore for a couple of days, but everyone was relieved to see me breathing on my own. Through the grace of God, one more goal was met, and the only thing left to remove was the feeding tube.

July 19 was a day that brought major milestones. Erin had her wisdom teeth taken out, and Mom went home to take care of her, leaving me alone for the first time since the accident. My friends in Commerce held a "Play *fore* Eric" golf tournament to help my family with the expenses of staying in Atlanta. With eighty-eight players and over two hundred hole sponsorships, it was a very successful event and was even covered by a local television station. My name wasn't the only personal touch. My jersey number was thirty-seven, and the tournament was held exactly thirty-seven days after my accident.

On July 20, I got news that my neighbor, friend, and fellow Georgia fan James Drinkard wore my South Carolina Gamecock hat and won the golf tournament. I may not have been there physically, but I was definitely represented.

True friends are one of the greatest gifts God gives His people. Proverbs 17:17 says, "A friend loves at all times, and a brother is born for adversity" (NAS). Friends made the long trip to Atlanta to visit us, pray for us, place "Pray for Eric" signs all over Commerce, raise money, and do everything they could think up to help. During our family's long days and weeks of adversity, our brothers and sisters were always there for us, sharing our burdens.

In the latter weeks of July, I began to struggle. Part of my problem was an infection, but there were questions about some of my medications, too. My physical and occupational therapists were concerned that the medicines made me sluggish and sleepy, keeping me on a plateau and stalling my progress. Although CT scans and x-rays showed that everything was healing, I began feeling more agitated and "stormy," as Mom calls it. The more conscious I became, the more spastic and restless I felt. A few days of trying different medications eventually got me back on track and improving again.

Working with the speech therapist still hadn't enabled me to talk. I could get out a word or two at times, but for the first time since babyhood, I was speechless. Coach Jarvis told me later that he regretted ever wishing I would just be quiet in his class. Seeing me unable to use my voice bothered him more than anything. Radio without sound wasn't Radio!

July 28 was the first day of football two-a-days to get ready for the 2003 season. I was supposed to be out there on the field, practicing with my teammates, sweating in the sun, and working to the point of exhaustion. Instead I felt like an oversized baby, trapped in an air-conditioned hospital and struggling to learn to eat, talk, and master all those simple life skills I'd taken for granted most of my life.

By July 29, I felt that about the only positive thing going for me was getting rid of my neck collar. My doctors told Mom and Dad that trying so hard in therapy was causing more muscle spasms, so they decided to try medication to help my muscles relax.

July 30—a release date. My parents were informed that I would be released on August 13 to go home. This pleased me but scared Mom; she was afraid I wouldn't receive the therapy I needed in Commerce. As always, she fought for me and got my release pushed back to August 20. At the same time, her faith came through to comfort her. Her journal says, "Maybe it was God's way of telling us you need to go home for a while."

By the end of July, we'd made progress in many areas on and off the scale. Our church, Mount Olive Baptist, had raised over $4,000 for our family with a ham-and-egg supper. We have pictures of John Smoltz, the Hall of Fame Atlanta Braves pitcher, visiting me at Scottish Rite. Now that's something I really wish I could remember! At this time I could spell my name, point out specific things like my name, the month, and the season, and give a "thumbs-up" to things I like. My weight was up to 111.4 pounds. I could make eye contact with people, but even with speech therapy every single day, I still couldn't talk—a major source of frustration for me and everybody else. In physical and occupational therapy, I worked on relaxing my muscles, increasing muscle tone, and improving my range of motion. My score on the Ranchos Los Amigos Scale improved to level five, indicating I was fully conscious but a little confused about my surroundings, having memory problems, and focusing on basic needs like eating and going to the bathroom. It doesn't sound like much, but that signified some major improvements.

On August 5, I took a step during physical therapy! While I needed help to take the step, I was able to support my weight and hold myself up. I was making visible improvements, and the CT scans showed my brain swelling had gone down.

On August 7, I was home for a couple of hours to complete a home-assessment test. I didn't care about the test; I just wanted to be at home—and not for just a few hours! John, my occupational therapist, and Jill, a therapist tech, rode with me in the Scottish Rite van. This was my first time away from my entire family since June 12. Two of the best things about being back in Commerce that day were (1) eating lunch brought in from Hart's, a favorite local restaurant, and (2) Dad letting my dog, Rudy, lick my face. John and Jill didn't bother to object. Although Rudy's licks wouldn't have met hospital sanitation standards, they sure were good therapy.

With my discharge date from Scottish Rite scheduled for August 20, it was important for everybody to see what preparations were needed to care for me at home. Our sports-oriented family had never thought about needing handicap accessibility, but then a major concern was whether my wheelchair could be maneuvered through the house. Holding our breaths as though that would make the wheelchair smaller, we made a trial run. We could get everywhere except through the door from the computer room to the kitchen. Whew! Dad was probably the most relieved, since he wouldn't have to do any major remodeling.

August 8, the first day of my junior year at Commerce High School. Without the accident, I would have driven myself to school, hung out with my friends, and gone to football practice in the afternoon. Of course, I was not really aware of this like Mom and my friends. With school starting, it would prove to be hard for them to visit me much during the week, but they could come on weekends. My communication was improving. I still couldn't talk, but I could make eye contact, point, gesture, and mouth a word or two. Mom gave me a bite of hot wings, one of my favorite foods. I licked my lips and give her a "thumbs-up," so they must've been stimulating to me.

My friend Moose came to see me when it was time to eat. I knew enough about what was going on to get upset at having anyone see my parents feed me. I pushed the plate away, made a noise, and got my point across. This is another example of how I was becoming more aware of my surroundings, and my parents were being sensitive to my feelings.

August 12 was the two-month anniversary of the accident. During physical therapy, they strapped me to a tall walker and let me stand up for thirty minutes! I put simple puzzles together with a little help and began to smile at people. My speech therapist helped me write my name. Never mind that it looked like something a chicken scratched in the dirt or a baby scribbled for the first time. I wrote it myself.

It was about a week before I was to go home. They fitted me for a wheelchair to take with me. According to Mom's journal, this upset her a lot, not because I had to be in a wheelchair, but because the salesman was trying to talk them into a wheelchair that would make things as easy as possible for me. This may sound mean and hard to understand, but Dad remembered the Grady doctor's warning and advice. He met with my Scottish Rite doctor to explain why I didn't need a fancy chair to make things super easy and why he and Mom didn't want me to have one. Athletes don't build strength by sitting quietly and taking life easy! I needed a basic chair to provide adequate support and reasonable comfort without tempting me to slack off my efforts to get out of it. Mom and Dad really wanted me to be comfortable, but not comfortable enough to be willing to stay in a wheelchair any longer than necessary. Their goals were to meet my needs and motivate me to work hard to get out of it! As usual, they turned it over to God, letting Him take care of it and getting the right chair for me.

***

ANGIE REDMON: Our biggest frustration was trying to strike a balance between how much help Eric really needed and how much we could push him to reach his potential. I didn't want a super-comfortable wheelchair—I wanted him to push himself to get better so he wouldn't need one. I understood that the others were trying to help by making his life as easy as possible, but I didn't want him to accept his current condition and settle for being less than he could be. I knew Eric would be mad at us if we didn't push him to work at getting better until he could figure things out for himself.

***

August 16. Commerce was still coming through for me, too. My friends from high school held a "Wash for Radio" car wash. They sold T-shirts and raised even more money for my family. More important than the money, though, these events encouraged my parents and eased some of their stress.

On August 17, Dad helped Erin move back to Clemson. She rearranged her schedule to have all her classes on Tuesdays, Wednesdays, and Thursdays so she could come home or to Scottish Rite on the weekends to work with me. This night was the first time Mom stayed with me overnight by herself. Mom's journal says we watched the movie *Pretty Woman*. I couldn't really follow the storyline, but the stimulation of trying to understand it was good for me.

In the days leading up to my dismissal from Scottish Rite, I made progress quickly. I became more relaxed in physical therapy and felt able to do the exercises easier. In speech therapy, I could put my lips together and follow simple commands. I could mouth the word "mom" and all of the vowels a couple of days before I was dismissed. Dr. Johnston was very impressed with my progress, especially when Mom used the communication board to ask me some questions. I could answer all of them correctly! Mom began to feel better about my coming home.

By August 20, I was home to stay! Coming back to "my town" was obviously a good move. In addition to excellent stimulation and therapy for me, our incredible hometown support team was making a big difference in my family's ability to meet my needs.

CHAPTER 5

BACK HOME

Fear not, for I am with you;
Be not dismayed, for I am your God.
I will strengthen you, Yes, I will help you,
I will uphold you with My righteous right hand.
—Isaiah 41:10 (NKJV)

Coming home turned out to be a significant step toward my recovery. Even though my family and friends did everything they could to make my room at Scottish Rite look and feel like home, actually being in our house apparently made a huge difference, and I started to gradually improve. That said, I still had a long way to go to get back to being myself.

Erin and I rode to Commerce in a special Scottish Rite transport van with attendants from the hospital. Mom and Dad followed in the car. Mom says the Scottish Rite folks were wiping away tears when we arrived at home. She thought something had gone terribly wrong, but the happy truth was they were deeply moved by what they saw in my town. From the time we left Interstate 85 until we got to my house, there were signs everywhere supporting me and welcoming me home. At first glance, you might think it was just before an important election because people's yards were filled with signs. Looking closer, you could read, "Pray for Radio" instead of "Vote for X." Store fronts had welcoming signs in their windows. Those attendants had never seen anything like this Commerce welcome. With all this support behind me, they told my parents they had no doubts I would recover.

Unfortunately, I couldn't sleep in my own bed or even in my room. I had to be in a hospital bed in my parents' room. Even though my eyes were open and I could follow things with my eyes, I still had a blank stare. With no emotions, no control of my body, and very little memory, I needed help doing everything.

Not being able to remember most of this is probably a blessing. There was a feeding tube in my side. I couldn't lift my head or hold it up, so my wheelchair had a tall head brace with a head strap. I had to sleep with special braces each night to correct the spasticity in my feet. Who would want to remember all that mess?

It wasn't long before I made visible strides to getting back to being "Radio." It was easy for friends to come by for visits, and I truly believe they stimulated me and my brain as much as anything the doctors and therapists did or prescribed.

Mom still felt afraid that coming home might've limited my rehabilitation and therapy. She, Dad, Erin, other family members, and really good friends made sure that didn't happen. My introduction to what we later called "redneck therapy" was just beginning.

First of all, they refused to modify the house just to make things easier for me. The only structural renovation was building a ramp going up to the back door. They were dedicated to helping me become independent again.

Dad turned our garage into a physical therapy room. He and Gary Tiller, my friend Hank's dad, built a huge therapy table to help me continue my stretching. Since he operates a cheerleading facility, Uncle Tommy was able to get a special mat for it. Later, Dad and our friends built other equipment because buying the professional models was too expensive. Although our insurance wouldn't pay for a standing walker to help me continue learning to walk, it didn't keep me from getting one. Dad took pictures of the kind I used at Scottish Rite and built one out of wood. Every night, he worked with me and stretched me. My friends began learning that if the garage doors were down, I was working on therapy and couldn't be disturbed. They respected that. It was tough love and I had to work hard, but it was the only way I could recover.

***

BOBBY REDMON: When we came home from the hospital, I was nervous. Were the doctors and therapists giving up on Eric? As soon as I saw how well he responded to being at home, I knew we had to figure out ways to keep him at home and keep going with his therapy. I also knew we needed some special equipment, and it was expensive.

I believe God gives all of us talents and expects us to use them. With help from family, friends, and neighbors, we built his equipment ourselves, and it worked.

With the garage turned into a gym, Eric called our therapy "redneck therapy." Like any athlete, he needed to be pushed to do his best, not babied. Even though he did most of the pushing, I hated creating the pain he endured from stretching those tight muscles. I think Eric would tell you today, though, that redneck therapy is the best therapy.

***

My therapy sessions at home included physical therapy, occupational therapy, and speech therapy. At this point, I still hadn't spoken even though I was beginning to mouth words more often. When my parents felt that the amount of therapy their insurance paid for wasn't enough, they hired a couple of private therapists to come in and work with me. One of them was a former Commerce quarterback: Kevin Poe.

***

KEVIN POE, certified physical therapist assistant: When I first began working with Eric, he was like a newborn baby. He couldn't talk or really communicate. His spasticity was the primary physical problem I saw right away. I approached him like a computer and started with the core issues. He had to relearn how to sit without falling, reach for objects, and do other simple things like that. One frustration was that I would stretch his arm out and his spasticity would just draw it back tight. It was really difficult to work through that. There were good days and bad days in the beginning. Any slight improvement would be celebrated by me and the family because at least we were seeing some progress.

Working on basic things like rolling, transferring weight, and other basic things were really time consuming. I would go to the Ronald McDonald House and work with him in their basement gym as well as in the Redmons' garage that his dad turned into a therapy room.

***

Leaving everything to the therapists isn't the Redmon way or the Commerce way. My family and friends worked with me, too. Erin was back at Clemson, but her schedule allowed her to be my therapist every Friday, Saturday, and Sunday. After working with me on the weekends, she went back to school on Mondays. I'll always be thankful that she gave up cheerleading for that whole year to help me get well.

Our primary goal was to loosen my muscles with stretching and to strengthen them at the same time. A huge goal for me was to hold my head up without any kind of help. I didn't like looking like a "bobblehead doll," and I was embarrassed that I needed a strap to hold my head in place.

My first few days at the house were hectic as friends came by to see me and welcome me home. They also brought my class ring to me. Even though I was unaware of it at the time, our family's friends were always thinking about us. Church friends brought supper for us every night so Mom didn't have to cook. They set up a schedule and took turns taking care of us. We had some professional therapists and home-healthcare personnel come in to work with me, too. Dad stretched me and helped me work out every night in the "redneck therapy room" he set up. He also took me to the living room and helped me get into my favorite chair, a green La-Z-Boy, so I could watch TV, especially college football.

After being home for a couple of days, my girlfriend, Sara Minish, came by for our first date since the accident. Although we hadn't been dating long enough to become serious, Sara was a loyal friend and booster. She had come to the hospital often and kept in touch with Mom on a daily basis. Although others were advising her to move on to other relationships, Sara was committed to helping me get well. She wrote me a letter for each day and delivered them in weekly packs so Mom could read one to me each day while I was at Grady and Scottish Rite. Now that I was home, she called and asked about convenient times to come over and visit. Sara went to another school, so our dates were always important because we couldn't see each other at school.

This night, she brought chicken fingers and a rented movie, which we watched together. I still wasn't fully aware of everything that was going on, and I sure couldn't follow the movie's plot, but I enjoyed having Sara there. All the encouragement and activities Sara and other friends offered were stimulating my brain, adding fun to my "redneck therapy" and helping me to come around to being myself again.

August 26 offered a major breakthrough in speech! Most people don't realize that our vocal chords are controlled by muscles. I had to rebuild and retrain mine before I could speak. My friends would bring me slushies when they came over. Those cold drinks probably stimulated my vocal cords and throat muscles as well as my determination to get well—another example of "redneck therapy."

For the first time since my accident, I actually spoke that day. I'd been mouthing words, but this was the first time I used my voice. I said, "Mama." Mom thinks this is the most important word I've ever said. I went on to talk for two or three minutes and told Mom I loved her. When I first started talking again, Dad got a little emotional. Worried because I couldn't figure out the difference between happy tears and sad tears, I asked, "What's wrong?" He fixed everything by explaining his relief that Radio's sound system was finally working again. Maybe I had been waiting until Erin went back to Clemson so I could get a word in edgewise without interrupting the constant chatter between her and Mom.

August 27 marked a whole week at home. Dad went back to work for the first time since the accident. Mom says she just sat out on the patio thinking about how good it was to be home and to see me making so much progress. I could make simple sentences, but just like learning to talk the first time, I wouldn't shut up. For example, whenever someone came over or did something for us, I would ask Mom, "Did you thank them?"—a totally unnecessary question because she always thanks people. Oh well, at least I could tell Mom that I love her!

***

DAVID "ATT" STEPHENSON, teacher and coach: My youth group at church was constantly praying for Radio and for his healing. They were his friends, and they wanted him to recover as badly as he did. One night we had been praying for his recovery and, more specifically, for him to be able to talk again. Adam Bagwell, one of Radio's teammates, led the prayer. After it was done, Adam asked, "Who would've thought that we would ever pray for Radio to talk?" Well, we all cracked up, because it was so true.

***

August 29–31. The most important things I would ever say started coming out, but they frustrated me and confused everybody else. Words were hard to find and I couldn't form sentences. I was saying words like "road," "Heaven," Papa," and "Greg." No one could understand what any of this meant at all. Then Dad and Erin tried to figure it out. Explaining stuff when you can't think or talk straight is tough. Trying to make others understand Heaven—how beautiful and wonderful and peaceful it was, who I had seen, why I wanted to stay there—was so frustrating. I could only repeat the same few words: "beautiful," "roads," "gold," "Papa," and "Greg." My family just looked puzzled. Mom thought I was talking about the road where I had the wreck.

Dad got it first and quietly said, "Angie, he's describing Heaven."

I said, "I love Jesus more."

Mom said, "We are supposed to love Jesus more, but I am glad God sent you back to be with me."

I said, "I didn't want to come back."

I tried harder to explain that she didn't understand what I meant. I wanted her to know that I loved her, but I loved Jesus more and wanted to stay with Him. Mom, Dad, and Erin tried really hard to understand what I was trying to say, but they just didn't get most of it. In her journal, Mom said that I was very emotional talking about it. The next day I repeated some of the same phrases to my friends.

My hospital records don't show a TDE (temporary death experience). It must have happened at my lowest point during those first seventy-two hours at Grady when I had the blood clots. I know for certain that I was in Heaven, and I remember some of the things and people I saw there, but it's hard to sort out the details and talk about them. I believe God allowed me to see Heaven so I could share my experience with others.

Besides the mechanics of talking, I was also relearning the names of simple things like the parts of the face. My friends came by to visit, quiz me to find out what I needed to learn, and then drill me on those things, just like you would teach a baby to talk. Because they worked with me constantly, repetition helped me to learn and to remember.

***

ANGIE'S JOURNAL: These are the words and phrases you have begun to use:

Perfect	*Great*	*I love you more*
Impossible	*Beautiful*	*No way*
Don't lie	*Always*	*Tell me a joke*
Full	*Thank you*	*Good joke*
Bad wrong	*Please do*	*Did you thank them?*
I'm confused	*Love to*	*Do you think I'm stupid?*
Soon	*I assume*	*My Lord*
Prayers work!	*I survived!*	*I love Jesus more!*

***

Dad went back to work in Atlanta, and Mom began working part time to keep our insurance. Since I couldn't be left alone and caregivers are expensive, God and Commerce bailed us out with volunteers. Mom set up a schedule for people to be at the house when they could work me into their schedules. My cousin, Michael, taught at the middle school. Since he didn't have a first-period class, he would come by to help me get up and dressed. All my clothes were too big for me, but that turned out to be a blessing—it was easier to get them on and off. Hank's mom, Vicki, and my Uncle Tommy came over a couple of mornings each week. On their days off, some of the firemen came, too. Teachers also came and read to me. The blessings of help just kept coming.

Things would've been a lot easier on my parents if they had made our house more handicap accessible, but they didn't want to make it too convenient for me to remain handicapped. They were willing to work harder in order to push me to get better.

Mom and Dad knew that God and our friends would be there to help us without even having to be asked. Not only did they help with my physical needs, they worked with me on speech exercises or drilled me with questions to the point that I would become frustrated and explode, "Do you think I'm stupid?"

About a week after getting home, I went on my first "field trip." My parents loaded me up, strapped me in, and took me to the Deer Trail Country Club where I had spent so many hours playing and holding down summer jobs. I don't remember the details, but I've seen the pictures, and according to Mom, I spent most of the afternoon telling everyone that I loved them.

Another major improvement for all of us came with regaining my speech. Finally! I could tell somebody when I had to go to the bathroom! This was the first step in getting out of my diapers, a constant source of discomfort and embarrassment. Since moving around was still difficult and slow, I had a few accidents, but everybody understood the importance of letting me push myself to get better. Although I used a little "pee jug" at times, the most encouraging thing for me was regaining some control over my body.

The next milestone was really simple, but I think it made everyone feel better. Aunt Debbie was leaving our house when she tripped and did a crazy little dance while she struggled to keep her balance. She looked so funny, I laughed out loud! No one had heard me laugh in so long that it caught them by surprise. Just like with talking, after laughing that first time, I wanted to laugh all the time. I began trying to get everyone who came to see me to tell me something funny and make me laugh. "Tell me a joke," became my next sentence. I was finally beginning to show some emotion and, slowly but surely, getting back to being "Radio."

***

To most people in the South, September means FOOTBALL! As my teammates prepared for their season opener, I was working at home, trying to regain my strength and flexibility. In my mind, I'd be back on the field with them soon. Even if every doctor told me that my football-playing days were over, I was doing everything I could to get back out there. Radio still didn't have an off switch! I learned to kick a football with both feet and I began to use my right arm. My left side was slower to recover, although there was slight improvement. I kept telling everyone, "I'll be back—I'm Radio!"

September 4 was the pep rally. One of the great traditions in Commerce is the downtown pep rally on the Thursday before the season's first football game. I went to the rally for a little while, and afterward a lot of friends came to our house, just like they did in the pre-accident days. Thursday nights always meant that some of my teammates, the Thursday Night Crew, would spend the night at my house. We always had a good time, and we still do.

***

CALEB JORDAN, friend: We were just high school kids and didn't put a lot of thought into the things we did, but we wanted to continue our tradition of getting together at the Redmons' house. We knew how much Radio loved being around others, so for him and for us, it was a way to keep things normal.

***

On September 5, Deanna Brown, the cheerleader who was supposed to ride to Moose's party with me on June 12, brought me a "goody bag" just like the rest of the players. I couldn't be with them because it was a road game—a tough pill to swallow! I hated to miss it, but

Dad grilled steaks and a few friends came to listen to the game with us on the local radio station. Hank intercepted a pass, and I wanted to call him right then and tell him, "Good job!"

Hank called me after the game to report that the entire team was playing for me. He made his interception for me, and the cheerleaders put my number on the banner the players ran through before the game! These friends were special.

Reading Mom's journal years later made me realize how hard it was for them to see me sitting in a wheelchair, listening to the broadcast of a game when I was supposed to be playing in it. At the time, I wasn't really aware of their feelings; I was living in the moment. As she wrote so many times, Mom was leaving it up to God. She knew He had a much bigger plan for my life.

September 6 was the day of armchair football. It was a Saturday morning, and Coach Savage brought me a copy of the game film on video tape. I didn't play, but I didn't miss the game after all. I was still a Commerce Tiger! After watching our Commerce game film four times, I watched on television as my South Carolina Gamecocks opened their season with a win. Sitting at home or on the sidelines watching football games instead of playing sure wasn't my first choice, but at least it's football.

Several friends came by during the evening and I was actually able to play UNO with them—not football, but at least it's a game, and I was playing instead of just watching. It may not sound important, but I am convinced that this kind of support and stimulation are just as important as the other forms of therapy I was struggling through. These activities helped me relearn things I lost and brought my personality back to being who I was before my wreck.

On Sunday, September 7, I went to church for the first time since the accident! This was a very special service for me and for my parents. My church family was so glad to see me in church again, and they showed it in many ways. They and the pastor did a lot of things that weren't part of the usual service: everyone stood and joined hands for a special prayer time for me, and a couple of friends sang a special song for me. There were smiles and hugs everywhere. It felt so good to get back and be a part of "the MOB" after being absent for almost three months.

September 11 saw me back with the Thursday Night Crew. My friends spent the night with me again. Horsing around and cutting up with them was great. I still slept in a hospital bed in my parents' room, but they stayed anyway and slept in my room.

September 12 marked the three-month anniversary of my accident, the first home football game of the season—a big day for me—and one of the most pivotal nights in my recovery. Dad told me I could go to the game under one condition: I had to work hard all week in therapy and get to where I could hold my head up without using the strap on my wheelchair. I did it! I worked hard and met my goal. There's just something about Commerce football that fires me up.

Everyone was excited to see how I'd do at my first game after the accident. The cheerleaders brought me a goody bag just like I was still playing. We started getting ready about an hour before the game. My neighbor James Drinkard helped Dad load me up, and then we were off. Dad drove up right behind the press box, unloaded me and my wheelchair, and took me into the field house and locker room for the first time since my workout on June 12.

I never dreamed I'd ever come in here in a wheelchair, but at least I was with the guys, feeling the excitement and the adrenaline. After visiting in the locker room, my cousin Michael, now assistant coach, pushed me out on the field and over to the sideline. As Mom described it in her journal, everyone stood and cheered for me while I waved back at them, just like I was in a parade.

Word had gotten out that I was coming to the game, so almost everyone was wearing one of the T-shirts various groups sold to raise money for me and my family. Five different designs were made, and the stands were filled with them. Who knew that years later I would occasionally see someone wearing one around town and thank God for this town and their support?

Tiger Stadium has a hill in the end zone nearest the field house. One of our great traditions is the Tigers "running down the hill" and into the stadium as the band plays "Tiger Rag." Once the team was on the field together, we knelt and prayed the Lord's Prayer. I was able to lift a prayer with my teammates once again. After the game, I told Mom that I hoped to be able to "run down the hill" one more time.

Dad and I watched the game from the Tiger sideline at one end of the field. I was excited because my Tigers were putting a whipping on Banks County. Dad said we'd stay for the first half, but I held up four fingers and insisted, "Football players play for four quarters!" At halftime, it was my job to pull the winning ticket for a raffle some of Erin's cheerleading friends held to raise money for my family. We stayed for the entire game as my Tigers won 35-14.

This was literally an unforgettable night, and not just because of the football game. It was unforgettable because it's the first complete memory I have of any event after the accident. I thank God for those memories. While I had hoped to recover more quickly, I felt convinced that I'd be back the next year to finish our senior football season with my friends.

Now that I was more conscious, more aware, and more talkative, Mom and Dad began noticing a new problem. One clue was my behavior while watching television. I would switch to the guide channel and leave it there for a long time, just watching the guide scroll through the different shows. My short-term memory wasn't working well at all, and I couldn't remember what television show was coming on what channel. I also asked the same questions over and over, repeated sentences, and had a hard time distinguishing shapes and pictures. When my speech therapist noticed it, we tackled this new challenge. It's a good thing football prepared me to deal with changing exercise routines. We added new exercises like playing memory games and using shapes to improve my memory and visual issues.

There was good news, though—my feeding tube finally came out, although not the way that it was supposed to. Kevin Poe, my physical therapist, was helping me to stand up when all of a sudden, blood goes everywhere! My feeding tube had tangled up in my gait belt and was pulled out. The fact that it came out during physical therapy was beside the point. It was out, and out for good! Other milestones included going to the computer, playing my music, and having my left hand begin to move better. Radio was coming back!

September 18 was an important day for two very different reasons. The happy reason is the Commerce Fire Department held a special Chicken-Q to raise money for my family, and we picked up their generous check. It seemed like every week someone or some group did something special like that for us. While insurance covered a lot of the costs of repairing and rebuilding Radio, there were many other expenses to be covered after the insurance had reached its limits. The extra physical therapists Mom hired to come to the house are just one example. These acts of kindness make me believe that, of all of God's gifts to us, true friends have to be at the top of the list.

The sad reason for the day's importance came with a telephone call later that night. While my Uncle Sam and Aunt Debbie were at our house, Sam helped Dad with my physical therapy. Shortly after they left, Uncle Sam suffered a massive heart attack.

On September 22, we went back to Atlanta for a checkup with my doctors. The big difference this time was that I was going by car, not by ambulance or van. I'd never been afraid to ride with Dad, because he's a very good driver, but at this point, being in a car in heavy traffic triggered irrational fears. I begged, "Drive safe! Drive safe!" over and over, and it must've bugged him to the limit. Sensing my anxiety and his distraction, Mom talked to me, trying to keep my mind off being in the car in Atlanta's notorious traffic.

At the hospital, Dr. Johnston said that I had improved to a six on the Ranchos scale—a major accomplishment from my level-two status when I first arrived at Scottish

Rite and my level-three or four status when I left on August 20. Impressed with my improvement, Dr. Johnston gave us a couple of options for the next phase of my recovery. I could either come back to Scottish Rite for a couple of weeks of intensive inpatient therapy or go to the day rehabilitation program. Mom and Dad said they'd need some time to pray about it before making their decision.

Overall, it was a good visit and something of an introduction for both of us. Because I was now fully conscious, Dr. Johnston heard me talk and laugh for the first time. I couldn't do either one when he worked with me as an inpatient. Later Mom and Dad took me down to the rehabilitation floor to see the nurses and therapists who had worked with me during the summer. They were excited to see me and hear me talk and seemed impressed with my overall improvement. Like Dr. Johnston, they now understood why my nickname is "Radio."

September 26, on the other hand, was a sad day. After his heart attack, Uncle Sam stayed in the hospital for several days but did not get any better. The family decided to take him off life support and let him go peacefully. He passed away shortly, and on September 28, we went to Uncle Sam's funeral at my church. My short-term memory problems were evident as I kept asking, "What happened?" throughout the service. A part of me is glad that I have no real memory of this or the next few days. Uncle Sam always played a special part in my life. He was one of my favorite uncles, and I loved him very much.

October 1. Back to school during a school day. Mom brought me to the field house, where several of my friends were taking weight training. Nobody will ever know how much I wanted to join them. My sad mood lifted, though, when Coach Savage presented my letterman's jacket to me. It felt great to put it on before going into the school. In the front office, I started laughing and told Mom that this was my first time being in the office without being in trouble.

October 2 brought two good firsts: a softball game and a local Mexican restaurant. It was the first time I'd been to a softball game or a restaurant since the accident. The noise and excitement of the game and the flavors of spicy Mexican dishes were extra good after all those months in the hospital.

October 3, though, was a bumpy day. I was making strides, getting closer to being the "Radio" of old, but I still couldn't walk, my left arm wasn't coming around like my right, and my short-term memory wasn't working well at all. More embarrassing was having some accidents at the table and not making it to the bathroom a few times. Maybe those bumps were God's way of pushing me to work harder. Based on these and other factors, my parents decided that going back to Scottish Rite as an inpatient was the best decision. That didn't sound so bad after they said I could stay home long enough to enjoy the homecoming game and dance. I didn't talk about it, but I was really tired of missing the fun and excitement of being a junior.

October 4 was the day of my send-off celebration. After church, my friends came over and held a "Send Radio Off" party. We weren't sure when Scottish Rite would call and tell us to come back, so we went ahead with the party before spending the next couple of days getting ready and waiting for the call.

As the football season continued, I went to most games, at home or away. The Thursday Night Crew spent the night before games at my house again—an ideal form of redneck therapy! Our neighbor, James, continued to go to the games with Dad to help load me up and get me out, a practical and much-appreciated example of "Love thy neighbor."

October 10 brought a road game. Dad and James took me to see the Tigers play Madison County for their homecoming game. Sara was on their homecoming court, and I took her a dozen roses (but with a Commerce Tiger ribbon). Their cheerleaders gave me a goody bag and told me that they had been praying for me, too.

A week later, on October 17, it was time for the Commerce Tiger homecoming! Fun, food, football, and a fall. This was my last day of redneck therapy before going back to Scottish Rite. There wasn't any school that day, so Mom fixed a big breakfast for me and the Thursday Night Crew to start the day off right. I was going to the homecoming game that night and the homecoming dance the next night.

Dad and James drove me to the school to watch the game. Being in the field house with the players during their pregame preparations made me want so bad to be dressing out, too! Coach Jarvis took care of me before the game so Michael could get his offensive linemen ready. He rolled me from the field house to the field to watch the team run down the hill. I was back with the Tigers, but not in the way I wanted to be. Once they got to the sideline, they all took a knee and Coach Jarvis rolled me into the huddle to pray the Lord's Prayer with them. Once the huddle broke up, he rolled me down to Dad to watch the game from the end zone, and I almost choked up. It was hard to accept not being out there on the field with my teammates, helping them pound Athens Academy 24 to 7. I felt determination to get back on the field with them by the next fall. Watching is good, but playing is a whole lot better!

At home after the game, I nearly scared my parents to death by falling out of my bed and cutting my eyebrow. Would these crazy accidents ever stop happening? Mom and Erin thought I needed stitches, but Dad bandaged it up good enough to stop the bleeding. I claimed to be okay because I'm tough as bricks. Going to the hospital was not a part of my homecoming-weekend plans!

The next day, October 18, brought about steaks and the homecoming dance. After sleeping in Saturday morning, I watched some college football, but my thoughts were on the homecoming dance. I couldn't just sit there when the music started! I wondered, *How in the world do you dance in a wheelchair?*

Sara couldn't go with me because one of her mandatory school activities was the same weekend. So, my friend Jade Klugh agreed to be my date for the dance. Mom cooked a great supper while Dad grilled steaks for Hank, his date, Jade, and me. That couldn't have been their first choice of a big dinner before the dance, but I really enjoyed and appreciated their company.

Time really does change things. Coach Jarvis and Erin volunteered to take Jade and me to the dance and look out for me. This time the year before, the idea of having my coach and my sister take us would have been inconceivable and totally unacceptable; now I appreciated it.

Once we got there, everything fell into place. I was able to get out on the floor, "dance" in my wheelchair, and have a great time with my friends. The plan was to leave early if I got tired, but I was having a ball, so we stayed for the entire dance. I even joked that being in a wheelchair made me the best one there at doing the "Tootsie Roll." It was another step in my frustrating and slow recovery. At least I was inching closer to being "Radio" again.

Scottish Rite finally told me to come back on Wednesday, October 22. I'd been home just over two months and had made dramatic improvements like talking, laughing, and carrying on conversations. Redneck therapy works wonders! At the same time, I realized there was a long way to go. I was still in a wheelchair, although I'd begun to take a few steps in the standing walker Dad built for me. My left arm and hand were still way behind the right side, and my short-term memory was unreliable. I hated to leave Commerce and the friends who loved, helped, and prayed so much for me and my family since the accident, but I knew those two weeks of intense therapy would be very important to my recovery. Hate it or not, it was time to go back to Atlanta and rebuild Radio. We had no idea the next phase wouldn't go as planned and unforeseen problems would complicate and drag out the process.

Me at three months old,
already in a football outfit

Playing football for
my first Tiger team

I was born a fireman.

Sophomore Tiger

Shoot! High School days!

"Keep your head down!"

Hanging out with Sis, my
Clemson cheerleader!

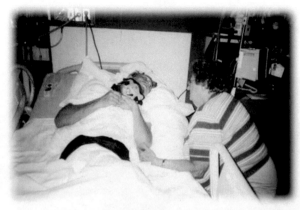

Visit from
my Nanny!

My family
and friends
at Camp
Commerce
at Grady

My first outing at
CHOA at Scottish
Rite. Still a ways
to go!

"Redneck Therapy" with Uncle TomTom and therapist

Kevin and Dad working with me

Support from Hank

Friends "washing for Radio"

"Play Fore Eric!"
Deer Trail Country
Club and Friends

Fire
Department's
"Chicken-Q for
Radio"

Me with others at Ronald
McDonald House

"Hey, Ronald!"

Headed to Day Rehab

I survived!

My cheerleader, Deanna, brings my Friday-morning goody bag by, even after my accident.

Welcome home from Lemarr Height neighbors Casey, Ann, Ansley, and Davis with me.

First day back at
Commerce High!

Prom with friends

Thank you, Ben Wilson, for
studying with me.

Erin back at school, and we're at
Clemson/SC game with family.

Me with my future brother-
in-law, Kyle

First time back at Tiger Stadium
with my team. Daddy and Drinkard
took me to team!

Thanks, Wes Massey! Wouldn't be here without you. Me and Wes at graduation.

With my family before graduation

With Mitch, Hank, and Caleb at a football game and at graduation. "A friend loves at all times, and a brother is born for a time of adversity" (Proverbs 17:17).

Receiving a phone call from Tommy Bowden, at the time the
Clemson head football coach, at the Ronald McDonald House. Erin
arranged this for me for Valentine's Day that year.

Star-94 radiothon
with Steve, Vicki,
and Tom Sullivan

Joe Nichols concert,
"The Impossible"

Having fun with the Boys and Girls Club of Commerce

My friend Gerald "Pro" Spear from the Deer Trail Country Club, where I hold my golf tournament every year

My donation from the Foundation to the Ronald McDonald House

My team of volunteers visiting the Team Radio room #217 at the Ronald McDonald House at Scottish Rite after delivering meals

With my good friend US
Representative Karen Handel

With NFL All-Pro DeAngelo Hall, who has become a
supporter and friend of my foundation

The big family beside the pool

The entire family at Erin's wedding

With Mom, Dad, Erin,
Kyle, and their kids

With YaYa

With Sandra Haggard
making caramel apples
for my Foundation

Putting the final touches on
the book with Jarvis

Speaking with Dad

With Hank in Las Vegas
for our thirtieth birthdays

Life's A Party setting up
graduation at the high school

Painting a fire hydrant in
downtown Commerce
with my neighbor Lynnly

CHAPTER 6

SCOTTISH RITE—AGAIN

I can do everything through Christ who strengthens me.
—Philippians 4:13 (God's Word)

October 22, 2003, brought me back to Atlanta and admission to Scottish Rite Hospital for the second time. My parents and I arrived early in the afternoon. The staff was happy to see me and excited to see how far I'd come in my rehabilitation. When I had left Scottish Rite two months earlier, I was unable to talk and was just beginning my physical therapy. Now I could talk, joke a little, laugh, and as Mom says, "put on a show." Scottish Rite was meeting the real Radio for the first time.

The overall plan for this visit was very simple. I was going to stay at Scottish Rite for two weeks and receive intensive therapy to improve my balance, strengthen my legs and voice, loosen the tightness in my left hand, and work on my short-term memory issues. My busy days began at seven o'clock in the morning and included speech therapy, occupational therapy, and physical therapy every day. Most of the therapists were the same ones who worked with me two months earlier, but I did have a new physical therapist.

One of the first things I used was the standing walker. Taller than a standard walker, it let me actually stand up and walk through the corridors, building up strength in muscles I hadn't used since the accident. The most important facet of using the standing walker, to me, was the fun I had as well as allowing my body to relearn how to walk. I felt great to be out of the wheelchair and actually walking around again, even if I was strapped to a walker. The first day I walked two hundred feet; a day later, I walked two hundred feet again, and followed that up by walking one hundred feet with a regular walker. Go, Radio! Go!

October 24. Pesky legs. I was up and walking, but my legs weren't behaving well at all. They kept crossing each other, making me step on my own feet in what's called "scissor stepping." I wanted so badly for my legs to work like they used to—like they were supposed to! I began feeling impatient with this whole rehab process and was so frustrated I exploded on Dad: "I'm pissed off at my legs!" My friend and homecoming date, Jade, came to visit me during the afternoon, the only bright spot in my day.

After meeting with Dr. Johnston, we learned about the decisions to use Botox on my inner and upper thigh muscles and to give me a flu shot since removing my spleen had made infections more dangerous for me. This was planned for October 30.

During this first week at Scottish Rite, my parents took me out to eat at The Cheesecake Factory. I ate and ate and ate while repeating, "Good food!" I ate so much I made myself sick, but it was worth it.

Sunday meant chapel service. We attended chapel at the hospital that morning, and the chaplain shared my story and my progress with being at home, combining "redneck therapy" with professional therapy, and being stimulated by friends and family. They sang one of my favorite songs, too: "I Can Only Imagine." The afternoon was filled with company from home, which was always good therapy and a nice break from hospital routines.

Back to professional therapy on Monday. We were trying hard to get my rebuilt body to work the way it used to. It helped to have something to do since all my friends were back in school, but my priorities were showing. Putting so much effort into physical rehabilitation was actually short-changing speech therapy involving my cognitive ability. My speech therapist worked more in that area, especially with my memory. First of all, she taught me to make little notes so I could remember things. As all my teachers could tell you, taking notes was never one of my strengths or practices, and it requires more concentration. This was a challenge for me, and it took time away from working on physical stuff. I confessed, as sort of an excuse to the therapist, "Well, I've never had a long attention span anyway." She required me to keep a journal and pick a current event to talk about every day. This was my "homework" for the next few weeks. Keeping that journal was a pain; talking about stuff was fine.

As my parents and I attended group sessions with other traumatic brain injury victims and their families, we became friends with several of them. We tried to help and encourage each other in our therapy sessions. One thing I learned is that while we all had traumatic brain injuries, we each had different challenges and required different types of therapy. I think these support groups helped all of us, patients and parents. Comparing our situations, we found that we weren't alone in our feelings; we all had similar frustrations and problems. Several of us from these support groups would continue to keep in touch through email and social media long after we left Scottish Rite.

October 30 brought with it problems. In the morning, I got nine Botox injections; after lunch, I got my flu shot. The results weren't in the plan or on the schedule. By evening, I had contracted the flu, or more accurately, the flu was hitting me like a Lincoln County linebacker. It was Thursday night, so the Thursday Night Crew came to visit me, bringing pizza and their usual high spirits, but I didn't feel well, and their best efforts couldn't make me feel better or get me into a good mood.

October 31. Halloween treats and tricks. I pushed myself doggedly through the morning therapy sessions and even carved a pumpkin for Halloween in occupational therapy. Missing the Commerce-Towns County game was disappointing, but knowing I could go to the game the next week against our biggest rival, Jefferson, eased the torment. Trying to help me feel better, my parents took me for a ride and milkshakes. Good intentions, but ultimately a bad call. My milkshake didn't sit too well on my stomach, and I immediately threw it up. The pain in my leg, meanwhile, felt as if it was getting worse, so I told Dad. We figured it was just sore from the Botox injections.

On Saturday, I had limited therapy sessions. My therapists were pleased with how well I did on the "arm bike," a passive-resistance exercise machine that has me "pedal" with my arms. I did it smoothly for five minutes. Later, watching the Georgia-Florida game, my parents quizzed me about the plays to build my short-term memory. Everybody was trying to help, but I felt that things just weren't working out. Mom looked frustrated, so I tried to reassure her by saying, "Don't worry, I'll be fine. God's got this."

On Sunday, I felt even worse. We said a special prayer in the chapel for my short-term memory and for the new kids who arrived. We hoped that by Monday I'd feel better and be ready to hit therapy hard again for one more week and then go home. Apparently, God had other plans and a different timetable. During the night, my fever spiked—a bad sign.

By Monday, I was body-slammed again! Unable to get out of bed, the doctors expressed confusion as to what was happening to me. My family felt scared and disappointed.

Tuesday was no better, and we were thrown for another loss. I was able to do a little therapy with my left arm, but my leg felt too sore to do anything. All the waiting and not knowing what to expect was tough; not getting back to physical therapy was worse. The fact that I couldn't do anything constructive felt like wasting time to me. I grumbled to the staff, "I came back for therapy, not to get sick."

Wednesday brought more busted plays. I didn't sleep well the night before and wasn't able to get out of bed all day. My leg was swollen, red, and sore. Thoroughly confused by this, the doctors ordered an ultrasound. I remained in bed and watched a couple of movies, *Forrest Gump* and *Sweet Home Alabama*—good movies, but I couldn't enjoy either and had a hard time remembering the plot.

That Thursday, we received bad news. The ultrasound showed a blood clot in my leg—a dangerous situation. The doctors said that this was very unusual; they'd never had a blood clot develop after a Botox treatment. Why did I have to be the first? Not only that, my upset stomach and throwing up caused reflux, so my stomach had to be scoped as well. With all of this, I began to feel like a practice dummy. I suspect Mom and Dad felt the same way, but they didn't say so. Instead of getting through with physical therapy that week and going home, I was stuck in the hospital, sick, and miserable. Even the Thursday Night Crew's visit didn't help much. I loved seeing them, but it just emphasized the fact that I couldn't attend the Commerce-Jefferson game the following night.

As an athlete, I've always loved Philippians 4:13. Paul wrote, "I can do everything through Christ who strengthens me." This ordeal broadened my understanding of the verse to see that it didn't just mean accomplishing great things in sports and in life. These challenges taught me that it also means handling the adversities that come our way. Even if I didn't like it or understand it, I had to turn this situation over to Christ and trust that this was all part of His plan.

By Friday, things were looking up. I felt better when I woke up, only to find out that special guests were at the hospital. They were visiting because Star 94, a popular radio station in Atlanta, was holding its annual "Care for Kids" radio-thon. I would get to meet some celebrities. What a great experience! Professional wrestler "Macho Man" Randy Savage was impressed that I wrestled, too. Caroline Rhea, an actress, comedienne, and television talk show hostess, encouraged me and my family. Incredibly, I was allowed to send a shout-out to the Commerce Tigers: "Play for Radio and beat the Dragons!"

That Saturday, we were on the radio! Dad, Erin, and I were all interviewed to share my story on Star 94. We joked about having "Radio" on the radio. I could never have guessed how God would use this experience. The next Saturday, the Cruse family—a football player from Dawson County, his sister, and their mother—came to visit me. After hearing my interview and story, he had told his mom that something about my story had touched him and he wanted to meet me.

Had my therapy gone according to our plans, I would have been back at home and missed the radio-thon. Instead, I participated in it and told my story. I couldn't have known it at the time, but as a result of that day's experiences, I would participate in the Star 94 "Care for Kids" radio-thon every year. This incident, more than any other, helped me to understand that God has a plan for me. I needed to turn everything over to Him and follow His plan.

Saturday brought more medicine and no therapy. I had been taking a blood thinner to get rid of the clot, but I couldn't do any therapy. I got a big lift when the Thursday Night Crew showed up to describe the game and deliver a cookie cake from Jefferson's cheerleaders. They had brought the cake to the game for me. I was glad the Tigers won the game and surprised about the cheerleaders. It meant a lot to know that these rival cheerleaders cared enough to get me a cake and to put my name on the banner they made for their players to run through. There is a bridge between Commerce and Jefferson, and there is a tradition of it getting painted the week of the game. Somehow my number thirty-seven was all over it in both schools' colors. The bridge may divide us in football, but it also helped to bring both communities together. Sometimes teens and cheerleaders get a bad rap, but experiences like these show how great they can be.

Sunday. Another week down the drain. I spent the day in bed, hoping the clot would dissolve and let me get back to physical therapy. Even lots of visitors didn't help much.

I experienced more disappointment on Monday. That no-good clot was still there. The doctors asked Mom if there was a history of blood diseases in our family. Medical science couldn't explain or fix it, so they wanted to blame it on my genes. I stayed on the medications and they drew blood to check levels. They drew so much of my blood, I played with the idea that they were secretly vampires! Although I knew Mom was really upset with all these problems and setbacks, she didn't talk about her feelings. Instead, she encouraged me by saying, "It's just another hurdle we have to climb."

Tuesday and Wednesday offered only more trials and tribulations. Same old story—stuck in the bed, unable to go to physical therapy, not making any progress. All I could do was "homework" assigned by my speech therapist to help my short-term memory and cognitive ability. I began pouring myself into that least-favorite aspect of my rehabilitation because there wasn't anything else I could do. Only later did I understand that the clot was the reason I started working so hard on the cognitive areas. Once again, God was using His plan to help me get better even though it frustrated me. To say I was upset would be an understatement. I was put on a new set of medications for the clot, and they included injections twice each day on top of the medications for my upset stomach. I just wanted to get back to physical therapy and being normal—not be a human pincushion full of pills and needles.

Thursday. Misery! I was so frustrated and upset that it made Mom worry about me. My planned two-week stay at Scottish Rite was now in its third week with no end in sight.

November 12 brought nothing to celebrate. On the five-month anniversary of my accident, I was back in a bed at Scottish Rite wondering if I'd ever get to finish physical therapy and go home. My bloodwork still wasn't right, and there were concerns because a filter hadn't been put in me earlier. Most TBI patients have this filter implanted to keep potential clots from getting to the heart. Because I had begun physical therapy so quickly in my first stay at Scottish Rite, it seemed unnecessary. My doctors and parents had believed that my physical activity sufficiently lowered the threat of a clot. Now, five months later, we wondered if that decision was a mistake.

In the meantime, I kept working on my speech and short-term memory and began showing improvement in both areas. My comprehension showed a lot of improvement, likely because the inability to do anything in physical therapy motivated me to work harder in cognitive therapy. I had to make progress somewhere! Even so, I told Mom how much I wanted to get back on my feet. The doctors kept telling me two things about my physical therapy: (1) I had to wait until the bloodwork was normal, and (2) I could maybe start back tomorrow. Mom was impressed because I could remember that, but how could I forget when they repeated it every day?

Thursday. Thank God for my Thursday Night Crew. They came to see me as they always did even though it meant driving to Atlanta and back. I was going to miss another game the next night and was not happy about it.

However, I had come to the conclusion that all of this was part of a bigger plan. I could only do what I could do, even if that meant working extra hard on cognitive therapy and my "homework"—without complaining about it!

Saturday. Progress! I was finally out of bed and eating some shrimp without throwing up.

Sunday. The bloodwork was back to normal! They said I could start physical therapy again.

Thanksgiving week was also the fourth week of my two-week stay at Scottish Rite! I felt ready to get back to work so I could begin day rehab. That meant I was also almost ready to go back to school.

The Monday before Thanksgiving was my first real day of physical therapy in ten days. We set up the schedule to go to physical therapy on Monday, Tuesday, and Wednesday and be at home in Commerce for Thanksgiving.

Wednesday. A breakthrough. Doctor Johnston was pleased with my progress concerning the clot and not walking with the scissors step, using a regular walker with a "gait belt," and the fact that my Ranchos scale level increased to seven out of eight. I still took two injections daily to get rid of the clot and had bloodwork done each week to make sure they were working. This would continue until the clot was totally gone, but Dr. Johnston released me from the hospital and I could ride back to Commerce in a car—no ambulance like last time!

At home with my family, friends, and dog, Rudy, on Thanksgiving Day, I felt most thankful to be alive, to be in Commerce, and to be able to see God's plan at work.

Friday, I was back with the Tigers! That morning a cheerleader brought me a goody bag for the Tigers' playoff game that night against Whitefield Academy. They made me an honorary captain, so I got to watch the Tigers win their first-round playoff game. Not being a real captain out there playing with them hurt. They were doing fine without me, but I didn't feel like I was doing so well without them. This was the first time a lot of my friends had seen me since I had left for Scottish Rite a month before. It was encouraging to see them surprised and impressed with how well I was doing.

Even with the clot setback, I saw things going in the right direction and my hard work beginning to pay off. Not only that, I was to begin day rehab on Monday. Most importantly, though, was actually learning to go by God's timetable, not mine, and to turn everything over to Him. I was beginning to fully understand what Paul meant when he wrote, "We walk by faith, not by sight" (2 Corinthians 5:7, ESV). Through frustrations and disappointments, I was learning that everything that was happening to me was a part of a bigger plan and that He was leading every part of my recovery.

CHAPTER 7

DAY REHAB
AND RONALD MCDONALD

For with God nothing will be impossible.
—Luke 1:37 (NKJV)

By Monday, November 24, I was back in Atlanta. We were living at the Ronald McDonald House and beginning outpatient day rehabilitation. My schedule was fairly strict. I worked from 9:00 a.m. until 5:00 p.m. each day. The goal was to get me ready to return to my school and community. I felt excited and ready to begin, and was looking forward to completing the program.

Our social worker helped us get into the Ronald McDonald House. We'd heard of this charity for years, but never really understood what it was or how it worked. Now we were getting firsthand experience. Dad was working in the Atlanta area so he and Mom could stay with me each night. Dad is quiet, reserved, and not very sociable, especially with strangers. He wanted us to stay in a hotel because it wasn't practical to make a round trip from Commerce to Atlanta every day. On the other hand, Mom has never met a stranger and will strike up a conversation with anyone, anytime, anywhere. We teased Mom that the deciding point for her was the plantation-style shutters. The truth is that once we visited the Ronald McDonald House, we all felt comfortable there and decided to try it.

We lived at the house in Atlanta from Sunday evenings until Friday afternoons and would go home to

Commerce for football games or wrestling matches and church over the weekend. Mom worked from home at this point. Conference calls enabled her to stay with me. Her bosses were really good about this because she needed to keep working part time to keep her insurance plan active.

Staying at the Ronald McDonald House was actually fun, almost like a house party. There were other families with teenagers living here, the most teens they'd had in a long time. Some were from nearby states like Alabama and South Carolina; others came from farther away, including one from California. Once again, I believe this was all part of God's plan so each of us could be there to support the others.

***

BOBBY REDMON: The Ronald McDonald House felt like home. Having my family together was very important to me. We could finally laugh and really enjoy each other's company again.

***

ANGIE REDMON: We had heard of the Ronald McDonald House, but really didn't know what it was. The second time we went back to Scottish Rite, we checked it out. I worried about whether Bobby would be comfortable there. Debbie and Tommy, my sister and brother, checked it out and assured us we would love it. They were right—it turned out to be a home away from home. While Grady felt clinical, cold, and full of gloom and doom, Scottish Rite and the Ronald McDonald House were warm and welcoming, giving us hope.

***

Supper each night was provided by various volunteers: a church, a business, a family, or an individual would donate the food. I enjoyed suppertime because all of us ate together. It gave us a chance to get to know one another and to help each other with our individual challenges. I knew Dad was a little uncomfortable in this setting, but he was willing to set aside his feelings because he could see the benefits for me.

My therapy sessions were specifically designed to prepare me for my return to school and to be independent and productive. My therapists tested to see exactly where I was in all areas so they could design the best program for me. They probably thought I needed charm therapy, too, because their testing and rehabilitation processes sometimes annoyed me. When I felt like they were asking silly questions, I would answer, "I'm not stupid!" I wasn't very interested in their cognitive therapy, speech therapy, or field trips to teach us how to be more independent. I would get frustrated because I didn't see myself as handicapped except for the fact I couldn't walk yet.

A typical day began with breakfast, and then we would take a shuttle bus to the rehabilitation facility. I was still in a wheelchair because I wasn't stable enough to use a walker all the time. Mom had to help me get around. I supposed this was her strength-building regimen since she no longer had time to go to a gym.

One of the first things we did at the center was group time with current events. Each of us had to watch or read about a current event and then share it with everyone else. This helped with socialization and short-term memory. My topics always centered on sports and *American Idol* because I could remember those topics.

After group time came occupational therapy, physical therapy, and speech therapy, all of which lasted until lunch. These folks were serious about rehab! Even lunch was a part of therapy. We had to eat without assistance to show the therapists what we could and couldn't do independently.

After lunch, I would complete some kind of educational testing with the testing coordinator. I flat out hated it! Basically, she drove me crazy with all of her questions; I knew the answers, but couldn't get the words out. I would get mad at the tester and frustrated with myself. Later, I realized this was a necessary part of my preparation to return to school.

Every afternoon we would review the day, which meant we had to use a calendar and a notebook or journal. I'd never been one to take notes in school because I didn't need them to pass. Before the accident, I either remembered the material or sat beside smart people and let them help me. Now I couldn't function without my day planner and notes.

We also had counseling sessions on how to handle some life situations that all teenagers face like sex, alcohol, and drugs. During these sessions, they began to see the real Radio and I got into trouble. For example, in a group session on drug use they said, "You can't smoke marijuana anymore." Just joking, I responded, "Oh no, I can't smoke my pot anymore?" Oops—they thought I was serious! The next thing I knew, they sent my parents all kinds of literature on the dangers of drug abuse and asked them to talk to me about marijuana and other drugs. This was worse than Coach Jarvis making me do jumping jacks until I was breathless in his history class.

After supper Dad would stretch me in the basement gym. Then we would go back to the group room with everyone else to watch television or play UNO until bedtime. This helped us rebuild both our thinking skills and social skills. It's funny how simplifying our lives into playing cards made such a big difference in our recovery.

There were some bad moments in rehab, too. For example, the doctors told me that I could never play sports again due to my injuries. I argued with them and swore that I could and would play again. Mom came to bat for me as usual. She believed my desire to play sports, especially football, was the reason I'd worked so hard to get well. She worried that taking that incentive away could make me slack off or give up. They also said I couldn't ride the Scream Machine at Six Flags. I didn't care about that, though. I've never liked roller coasters anyway.

Like it or not, I was steadily becoming more aware of what a traumatic brain injury really is and how it would affect the rest of my life. That was definitely not happy news for an athlete. I was also learning how to avoid getting another TBI and how to pace myself. A day of therapy would leave me physically and mentally exhausted. I had to learn when to push myself and when to back off. If I didn't rest and give my brain and body needed breaks, they would just shut down.

My first week in day rehab at Scottish Rite was primarily one evaluation after another. There really wasn't a lot of actual therapy because they wanted to see how I settled in, where I was, and what I needed to improve. One positive thing about day rehab was that Sara Beth, one of my friends from my earlier stay at Scottish Rite, was there, and we were able to work together some. God had brought our families back together to support each other.

On one Friday afternoon we went to Commerce's state football playoff game at Hawkinsville. The Tigers and the Redmons did not get a warm reception—it sleeted and snowed! Before the accident, that wouldn't have bothered me; I always ignored getting wet and cold as a water boy. Now, I was freezing to death! Commerce moved the ball pretty well, but only scored once and lost the game. One of their best players was Charles Johnson, a defensive end who went on to play for Georgia and the Carolina Panthers. It hurt to think that maybe if I could have played, the outcome would have been different. I sympathized with my friends because I was sorry they lost. I then promised to be back to help them the next year when we would be seniors.

Weekends at home always felt too short. My friends came see me on Saturdays. We would watch football, but I also had to maintain my workout schedule. To help with this, my parents arranged to have a therapist come to our house to work with me. On Sundays we would go to church, eat lunch, and then we would return to the Ronald McDonald House and Scottish Rite.

I began day rehab's second week on December 1. We saw the results from those annoying evaluation tests I completed the previous week. Mom was really upset to see how far I still had to go. No matter how much discouragement she felt, she would try to hide it from me and put a positive spin on it. Mom would always tell me to keep working no matter what happened or what anyone said.

My therapists saw my lack of focus and short attention span as problems. On the other hand, Mom saw them as positive signs that I was getting back to normal—*my* normal, not textbook normal. These have always been issues with me; she knew they weren't part of the TBI stuff.

The second week brought a bigger pain than extra laps after a hard practice—more homework. We read stories, reviewed journals, and did simple math that Dad would help me with. Unlike Erin, I'd never been much for "sit down and study," and I definitely didn't like it now. (Writing *Life's a Party* years later had us joking that it took smacking my skull and a TBI to make Radio write a book.) On the good side, I was eating more, gaining weight, and getting my cell phone back so I could talk with Sara each night. She was a bright spot even in dark times.

Getting closer to Christmas, we settled into a nice routine, and I felt like I was improving every day. They said I'd be done with day rehab at the beginning of February! Isn't it strange how a few months in the hospital could make going to school look good?

Coach David "Att" Stephenson, my defensive back coach in football and the head golf coach at Commerce High, came to Atlanta every week to visit me. Coach Att's brother is Coach Jimbo Stephenson, my middle school football coach. He was a very important part of my rehabilitation and transition to life outside the hospital because he knew what I was like and what I could do before I was hurt. Coach Att encouraged me and shared a lot of information with my therapists to help them work more successfully with me. This helped to keep me out of trouble when the therapists didn't understand that joking is a part of my personality and my way of dealing with difficulties.

***

DAVID "ATT" STEPHENSON, Eric's former coach: I got to know Eric when I moved back to Commerce in 2000. My first impression was that he was a very nice, polite kid. I called him Eric, and didn't understand why everyone called him Radio. After being around him a little while, I came to understand the nickname better. The only difference between Eric and a radio was that you could turn a radio off. He was still a nice kid.

The night before his accident, I asked if anyone would volunteer to help me with recreational activities at Vacation Bible School starting the next week. The first volunteer was Eric. He also volunteered his sister, Erin. She told me later that he had come in that night and told her she was helping Coach Att the next week. That was just Radio—he loves to help people.

I don't remember a lot about my experience at Grady. When I went to see him the morning after his accident, he was all curled up. That scared me because I had coached a kid in Thomaston who had a car accident. He had curled up in a fetal position just like Eric was. That young man didn't make it. When I saw Eric, I didn't think he would make it either.

I don't remember ever being the official liaison between Scottish Rite and the school. I started to visit him once each week and got to know his therapists quite well. Dr. Susan Galis, our director of special education, asked me if I would be willing to help Eric with his schoolwork when he came home, and I agreed.

***

Changes came before Christmas. Aquatic therapy started twice a week; water's resistance helps with spasticity and relaxation. This sure was different from swimming at Deer Trail! They also gave me Ritalin to help me focus better and a regular walker instead of the wheelchair to go from class to class. I named it my "Papa Walker" because it made me look like an old grandpa. About this time, a few therapists expressed concerns about things I had said in my classes. They reported to my parents that some of my comments were inappropriate and rude, but they didn't give any examples. Because the therapists had warned Mom and Dad that TBI patients sometimes start cussing, even though they didn't before, they worried that I might be cussing or being disrespectful, behaviors not tolerated in the Redmon family. Talking about it as a family was confusing because none of us understood what the therapists meant. I didn't think I was saying or doing anything wrong.

Coach Att to the rescue! He solved the problem by observing me in my classes and therapy sessions. As my friend, he saw that I was just being myself and convinced everyone that they were finally seeing "the real Radio" — a nice kid who is always cutting up and joking around, not a smart-mouth teen being rude or disrespectful. For example, using the phrase "Papa Walker" to describe my walker upset some therapists until he explained that it was my way of using humor to cope with my situation. I'm thankful that God sent Coach Att to help us through this period.

***

DAVID "ATT" STEPHENSON: Some of the staff had told me that Eric had been difficult and a little disrespectful at times. I know Eric doesn't have a disrespectful bone in his body. Once I explained that this was his personality and that he was just trying to be humorous, they began to understand him better. Before long they were telling me that now they knew what he meant—and he was hilarious. I believe that they had never seen a patient quite like Radio before.

***

Another controversial issue sounds silly, but I believed I was in the right. One therapist had asked me the same question at least a hundred times—it seemed more like a thousand times! I answered her question correctly every time, but she disagreed. She would ask, "What do rabbits eat?" and I would answer, "Corn."

Now, to most people, that may seem ridiculous, but it's the truth according to Radio. The irresistible force was colliding with the immovable object because she thought I was having problems "processing" the question. I knew she wanted me to say "Carrots" because it was the word on her answer sheet, but I wouldn't say "Carrots" because it wasn't the answer in my experience. She didn't know I fed corn pellets to my pet rabbits, and I was too stubborn to explain or to change my answer. Stalemate! It drove Mom crazy that I wouldn't just answer "Carrots" to satisfy her. I'm Dad's son and I don't change answers just to please anybody.

The holiday season was tough because I only had a few days off from rehab. Fitting our shopping, family holiday meals, and other activities around my therapy schedule was difficult at times. Mom found it especially hard to go shopping because she saw mothers with their healthy sons walking around, carrying packages, etc. like I used to do. Dad kept his feelings to himself.

During this time we shared one of Mom's biggest moments. For the first time, I remembered the three colors in the order she told me the night before: red, green, and blue. She was excited because it showed her my short-term memory was improving. Of course, I didn't tell her that I knew because she had used the same order of the three colors every night for months! Still, the fact that I memorized and recalled the three colors was a step in the right direction. Another positive sign was my weight, up to 137 pounds from its low point of 106 pounds after the accident.

On December 19, we enjoyed our Christmas tree at home. For once, there was no company—a rare and enjoyable occurrence. Dad and I watched some of the state football playoffs on television.

December 20, however, saw a family divided. Mom and Erin went to her family's Christmas celebration at Aunt Debbie's house while Dad, James, Casey, and I went to the Class A state championship football game between Lincoln County and Hawkinsville.

December 21 was a great day. Sara spent the day with us. Everybody, especially me, was pleased that I could use my "Papa Walker" and actually walk into church with her. After lunch we exchanged Christmas gifts: a shirt and a CD for me; a sweater, perfume, and a necklace for her. It felt so good to share quiet, happy times with Sara. Then it was back to working out and returning to Atlanta's hustle and bustle for two days.

December 22 had two good surprises and no bad ones. The doctor who was treating my stomach problems released me. The Cruse family from Dawsonville who had visited me after the radio-thon came back to see me. Everybody was happy about my progress.

December 23 was the start of Christmas break. We had a couple of days off. They let me bring my "Papa Walker" home to keep up my practice using it. My hematologist was way behind schedule, so we were late leaving Atlanta. The traffic was awful. We met the Tillers for supper at T-Bones in Commerce, and seeing gift-bearing friends at home made things better, but I was really tired, which messed with my short-term memory. The best Christmas present I could get would be improving my short-term memory.

December 24. Christmas Eve. Our family tradition is to go to a movie, but this year we decided to stay at home. Many friends came by to see me and brought tons of gifts. I joked that I would go into a coma again the following summer if it meant that many more gifts.

December 25. Like old times, our neighbors, the Drinkards and the Warnells, came for breakfast. My parents' gifts to me included a karaoke machine and a new cell phone. They hoped singing and talking would strengthen my voice and my projection. This kind of therapy was fun! I tried them out quickly, calling friends to catch up on the Christmas news and even "singing" the instrumental parts of songs by holding the word "instrumental" as long as I could while the music played. I think the karaoke machine and cell phone helped rebuild my "sound system," and they became my favorite therapy.

December 26–28 were really laid-back days. Redneck therapy, friends stopping by, enjoying my gifts, a visit to Deer Trail including a ride on a golf cart, schoolwork, a big improvement in my walking . . . and too soon, it was back to the Ronald McDonald House.

I went back to rehab on December 29. The hematologist said everything was fine, no problems with the blood clot, although I still had to take two injections each day. It was a miracle my skin didn't leak after being stuck so many times! In rehabilitation classes I did more reading and writing as well as fractions in math. Rehab was becoming more like school every day to prepare me for the real thing. Counseling sessions continued to help me face the pressures of being a teenager as well as with my TBI issues. Erin was home from Clemson and went to counseling with me a lot. It's a good thing she was with me when I made that joke about smoking marijuana. Erin was the one who had to explain to my parents why my therapist thought I was a pothead.

December 31. Therapy, celebration, and the end of the worst year of my life. The *Commerce News* ranked my story as one of the top five that year. I would've preferred to not be on that list. In all honesty, though, the story was not about me, but about the reaction of my friends in the city of Commerce and how they rallied to help me and my family.

After therapy on New Year's Eve—not my first choice to start celebrating!—I went home and spent some time at Hank's house. Our family had fun bringing in 2004 with the Tillers. I was glad to have 2003 in my rearview mirror.

January 1, 2004, felt almost like old times. I spent the day watching football, the same thing I had done every year. Of course, Dad helped me exercise, but for the most part, I watched every game I could and then got ready to go back to Atlanta for the final big push in therapy. Well, I thought it was final, but all too soon I would find out it was going to be a lifelong thing.

January 2. Scottish Rite and those same old frustrations. All I wanted to do was walk—that's it. I didn't care much about cognitive therapy, speech therapy, and all those other therapies. I just wanted them to please let me focus on the motor skills and physical problems and not worry me about the brain things.

It was very discouraging when they started testing to see if I could walk backward or back up with my walker. I couldn't do either one, and I didn't understand why. It seemed so simple, but I couldn't do it to save my life. To complicate things, my therapy was including more and more "schooling," and it wore me out to the point that I didn't feel up to working on walking. Like the time I had the flu and the blood clot, this was one of my few really discouraging times.

Cognitive therapy—the good, the bad, and the ugly. One positive aspect of my cognitive therapy was experimenting with my Ritalin dosage until the doctors felt like I showed improvement in focusing. I was never one to focus on anything for any length of time before my accident, so any help in this area was appreciated, at least by my teachers and parents.

There were academic frustrations, too. I had to write a paragraph telling my sister how to make a peanut-butter-and-jelly sandwich. In my opinion, it was a crazy assignment. Then, I realized she had no idea how to make one. She put the peanut butter and jelly on the same piece of bread. Everybody knows that you put the peanut butter on the left piece of bread and the jelly on the right piece! Or, you can put the peanut butter and jelly in a bowl and mix it together—that's the best way. I then had to write a paper on someone who had helped me. Coach Jarvis was my choice. Erin made me rewrite that paper several times until every bit of my patience was gone. I exploded and told her that I wasn't perfect like her, and that my paper wasn't ever going to be perfect.

The really bad news was having to pick a topic and write a paper every weekend for homework. Man, I hated that worse than running extra sprints on a sweltering August afternoon. Looking back, I realize the therapists were trying to make me use my processing skills and logical thinking. Yet at the time, it just felt like they were torturing me. I kept praying that it would all make sense soon, that my patience would hold out, and that my faith would be fulfilled.

Football season was over and wrestling season was well under way. I love wrestling almost as much as football. It's a one-on-one true test of your strength, skill, and stamina. I loved being on the mat and having to do everything all by myself. At the beginning of my journey to recovery, I thought if I couldn't get back for football, maybe I could get back for wrestling. Now I was beginning to realize that wasn't going to happen, either. Another unexpected body slam.

January 10 was my first wrestling match. My goal was to walk into the gym by myself with my "Papa Walker." I sent my parents in ahead of me and then walked in on my own. Everything seemed to stop in the gym while everyone cheered for me.

For some reason, I felt I had to explain to head wrestling coach Joe Hames that therapy would keep me from being at every match. I guess the feeling came from years of training that you don't miss games or matches; he understood my feelings. Coach Hames allowed me to be a captain at every match I attended. They waited for me to walk out, and then I would get to flip the red-and-green flip disk before each match. Fridays were always my best days because I went home to Commerce and the wrestling matches over the weekends.

On January 13, 2004, they fit me with ankle/foot orthotic braces to help with my drop foot problems. These things were ugly, high-tech replacements for the Ace bandages and tape my school athletic teams used to support weak ankle and foot muscles. They were fitted to my feet and not hinged so they could keep my feet from dragging when I walked. I hated them because they were uncomfortable and hot.

January 14. Brain facts and transitions. My brain awareness class played a major role in understanding rehab. I'd never thought about how much my brain controls. Basically, it controls everything; brain failure equals mind and body failure. It's no wonder my TBI made me such a train wreck.

Coach Att and the therapists discussed how to begin my transition back to school. He observed me in my classes at Scottish Rite and explained how being at Commerce High School could help me. For the first time returning to school seemed real—I honestly believed I would be going back to school soon. My faith was finally paying off and my prayers were being answered! Now I knew I would eventually be able to do anything I wanted—well, anything within reason. Playing active physical sports wasn't ever going to happen again. Dad and I went out for a milkshake to sweeten that painful realization. After dinner we enjoyed karaoke night at the Ronald McDonald House.

January 15. Eye check. An eye specialist tested me to make sure that everything was fine with my eyesight. What a relief to find out that my vision was perfect. At least one part of me survived intact and didn't have to be rebuilt!

Mom said I was the life of the party the night before. I guess I couldn't control my excitement at singing with and for the other kids. While my physical recovery was taking a while, my personality was coming back. I felt good about where I was.

January 17. Cheerleading competition. Just like the old days, we drove to Atlanta to watch the cheerleading competitions at the World Congress Center. I was glad my vision was good because those girls looked great. Hank and his family were with us. We had a great time, and we didn't get home until after midnight.

January 18 was Dad's birthday. Erin was back at the cheerleading competitions, so we'd give him his presents either that night or the next morning. We actually decided to stay home from church and rest. This was something very new. Being tired from staying out late Saturday night would never have been an adequate excuse to miss church before my accident! Even so, you best believe that being dog tired wasn't excusing me from therapy. Dad still stretched me three times.

On January 19, we celebrated my birthday early. Eighteen of my friends had lunch with me at a local Mexican restaurant to celebrate my seventeenth birthday. Others came by our house later in the afternoon. Back at the Ronald McDonald House, we cooked steaks and celebrated with my new friends there, too. It was a great day, but I missed my usual birthday party with the cheerleaders.

January 23 brought good news! The doctor checked my blood and the clot proved to be almost gone. We scheduled an ultrasound in a couple of weeks to make sure it was really gone. My weight was back up to 142 pounds, so I celebrated my physical recovery as well as my birthday that week.

January 24. Progress! My stamina had increased—we went to a cheerleading competition in Winder that morning and to the wrestling matches in Dacula in the afternoon. I didn't do much therapy, but that's okay. This time it was by choice, not because of setbacks. It felt good to spend the day supporting my friends who had supported me.

January 25. Saved by bad weather. This morning was cold and rainy, so Mom and Dad went to church and Erin stayed home with me. The weather got worse during the afternoon with freezing rain in the forecast. Dad decided to take me back to Atlanta early. Mom teased that Dad and the weather were rescuing me from an awkward situation. My unreliable short-term memory had led to a big mistake. Brittany, an old friend I had known since preschool, had invited me out to eat. She went to a different school and wanted to see how I was doing. I forgot I already had a date scheduled with Sara. This was a social fumble with possible consequences as bad as my infamous fumble that cost our team a touchdown when I had tried to show off by switching hands. Going back to Atlanta early let me cancel both invitations without making a mess. Once again, God came through!

January 26–31 was a whole week of progress in therapy with no setbacks. Life was feeling good.

February 1, 2004. Super Bowl Sunday and a victory for me. I walked into church with my "Papa Walker." At the end of the service, Pastor Tyson asked the congregation to offer forty days of prayer to improve my walking and memory. Mount Olive Baptist Church truly supported us in every possible way.

We went back to the Ronald McDonald House early so that we could watch the Super Bowl. When car problems stranded one of the Ronald McDonald House families from Tennessee, Dad was able to help them fix their car and go home. He said it felt good to repay some of the kindness we received from our friends and neighbors. I enjoyed watching the Super Bowl and told Mom, "I love football!" As if she didn't know that!

February 2. Great news. At rehab, I learned that my graduation from Scottish Rite would be on March 5. Finally! That meant the month of February would be very important and very busy. We planned field trips out in the community to make sure we could handle it. We had to plan budgets, go shopping, and actually buy what we needed. Some of my friends at the Ronald McDonald House were also going home. I'd miss them, but felt thankful we'd improved enough to leave. Now I was just one more month from being ready for school in Commerce.

February 6. "Goodbye, Granny Ma," and "Hello, quad cane." One of my favorite friends at the Ronald McDonald House graduated today. Julie and I cut up together a lot. She called me Granny Pa and I called her Granny Ma. Our jokes and nicknames helped us and the others to laugh even when we felt more like fussing or crying.

In therapy I walked up to three hundred feet with my walker, learned to walk up and down steps, and transitioned to a "quad" cane. Quads have four short legs at the bottom for extra help with balance—I absolutely didn't need a fall now. The AFO braces on my ankles helped, but I hated those ugly things. TBI or not, appearance is important, so I told anyone who'd listen that those braces made me look stupid. Overall, my walking was improving, but my right hamstring still wasn't working right. The doctors decided to use Botox again to weaken the larger muscles in my leg and force the smaller ones to work harder—a scary thought.

I was improving academically, too. My writing speed was faster, my reading comprehension had improved, I could carry on conversations, I was using bigger words, and I could talk in complete sentences. Radio's "on switch" was "on" again! Mom kept telling me that Mount Olive's Forty Days of Prayer were working and I should keep working on my end. She didn't have to tell me that because I was already working as hard as I could to get ready to go back to school. The Ronald McDonald House is a great place, but it wasn't in Commerce and it wasn't home.

I loved going home on weekends for the wrestling matches and to see my friends. I made it to the last wrestling match of the regular season. Now I was looking forward to the state playoffs and duals. My parents were looking for a place to continue my physical therapy once I left Scottish Rite and started back at school. They chose a place in Athens and set up a schedule so I could go to therapy three mornings each week without missing classes at school.

February 12. Hallelujah! The ultrasound on my leg showed that pesky blood clot was gone, vamoosed, totally out of the picture. NO MORE SHOTS! I almost danced up to the fourth floor to see Dr. Johnston and his staff. Excited and glad to hear that I was almost ready to go back to school, they rejoiced with me.

Valentine's weekend. I stayed put for the weekend. Mom and Dad decided to remain at the Ronald

McDonald House to rest. Going home is always a whirlwind of activity: wrestling matches, out to eat, church, and friends coming over to our house because it's the only chance we get to visit. My parents figured that staying at the Ronald McDonald House for the weekend would give us a much-needed break. It wasn't our traditional Valentine celebration, but this hadn't exactly been a traditional year. Erin's Valentine's Day gift was persuading Clemson's football coach, Tommy Bowden, to call me. Even though I'm a South Carolina fan, talking with Coach Bowden was a pleasant surprise. A peek into the future would show that in a couple of years, Coach Bowden and I would both speak at a Fellowship of Christian Athletes dinner in Commerce.

Dad and I went to the state wrestling duals while Mom and Erin shopped. Since a lot of my friends had recovered enough to go home, new kids had moved into the Ronald McDonald House. There weren't as many teenagers, we didn't know each other very well, and we didn't do much after dinner except play some cards—not exactly a weekend to remember.

February 20. Commerce High School was getting closer! While Coach Att came to talk about my coming back to school, my teacher's report included, "Eric can focus for forty-five minutes now." She was proud of my progress, but I thought it was funny and couldn't resist joking, "That's forty minutes longer than before my accident!" Coach Att gave me a knowing smile.

When I worked on budgets or went shopping, I usually needed minor assistance. I had learned to be more organized and to use those skills to help me remember things. My teacher recommended using a recorder in class as a memory crutch and keeping a thesaurus with me so I could find suitable words when I got stuck. While I hated using all these cognitive props because it made me feel like people would think I was stupid, the skills and tools would really come in handy in the future when I started my own businesses. God was working His plan even though I wasn't usually aware of it and had to accept it on blind faith.

February 25. From walker to limo! I took the shuttle without my wheelchair. I used my "Papa Walker" the entire time. This was the first time I did that, and even my bus driver was proud of me. I wouldn't admit to anybody that walking wore me out.

We arrived in style at an Atlanta Thrashers hockey game that night. A limo picked us up from the Ronald McDonald House and drove us to Philips Arena for the game. The fans were still sad that one of the Thrashers had recently died in a car accident. I mentioned to Mom that it was ironic his hockey jersey number was thirty-seven, the same as my football jersey number. I saw this as another reminder of how blessed I was to be alive and getting back to my old self.

February 26 was a strange day. It snowed in Atlanta, so the shuttle bus couldn't run and I couldn't go to therapy, but I could sleep until almost lunchtime. I did some homework, but not much else. This was probably a good thing because neuropsychological testing was scheduled for the next day.

February 27. Fun Friday! Being rested probably helped me to focus on the testing, and it went well. Back in Commerce, I spent the night at Hank's house. My parents were scared to death because it was my first sleepover since the accident and my first night without at least one of them in my room. They agreed to it because they knew Hank's mom, Vicki, had spent so much time helping take care of me that she knew how to do things for me as well as anyone.

Mom's family treated Mom and Dad to a weekend at Chateau Elan. They enjoyed going to the spa and having a relaxing evening after all those stressful days and nights in Atlanta. I enjoyed knowing they were having fun and not being the "helicopter parents" my accident forced them to be.

My final week in day rehab was busy, but seemed to drag on forever. I felt so ready to go back to school with my friends! On Tuesday, a staff member from the high school came to make plans for my return. I had finished all the exit testing and preparations to return to Commerce High School.

Friday, March 5. Graduation, excitement, and celebrations! Mom and Dad hired a limo to take me home, a much quieter, more comfortable ride than the med-evac helicopter that brought me to Grady. I had come a long way since that flight on June 12. Looking back, it seemed like it was the beginning of an impossible journey. Athletics and faith, however, had instilled a "never-quit" attitude in me, and now I could see the results of all of our hard work.

Several family members and friends came to Atlanta for my graduation from rehab. I was nervous, but I gave a speech and sang "The Impossible" by Joe Nichols—my theme song and inspiration. I listened to it and sang it countless times during those long days of R & R (recovery and rehabilitation). The second verse is about a young man who has been told he would never walk again after a car accident. Through hard work and determination, that guy made it—a clear message to me to keep trying in spite of setbacks and discouraging diagnoses. If he could do it, I knew I could do it with God's help! The most important line from the song for me is "I've learned to never underestimate the impossible." When I sang, they got all emotional, and some of them cried. Now I could recognize happy tears—thank goodness! Everyone told me I did a good job on my speech.

After the graduation ceremony, my friends rode with me in the limo to a party at Mount Olive Baptist Church in Commerce. Over two hundred more friends and a huge party with cakes, speeches, and even T-shirts that said "I Survived Day Rehab" were waiting there for us. I realized again that I was blessed to have such an awesome God and so many loyal friends. The next week I would be going back to school with them. As scared as Mom was for me, I knew I was ready.

***

TAFFY CARRUTH: When Eric came home from rehabilitation, I was one of several hundred people standing outside Mount Olive Baptist Church awaiting his arrival. Before long, he arrived in a white limousine. The crowd cheered as Eric stepped out of the limo with a walker and greeted everyone. We were really happy to see him. He had come a long way from lying in that hospital bed at Grady. When Eric came over to me with the help of his walker and said, "Thank you for saving my life," I cried!

CHAPTER 8

"GIVE ME A CHANCE!"

*Greater love has no one than this, than to lay
down one's life for his friends.*
—John 15:13 (NKJV)

March 8, 2004, saw me back at Commerce High School. It had been nine months since my accident—a grueling round trip from being a sixteen-year-old athlete to being like a helpless infant to returning to high school as a junior and seventeen-year-old. I was excited to be going back to school and being with my friends. I'd been preparing for this since my recovery began, but I would be lying if I didn't admit my feelings were mixed. Confidence and faith told me I'd be fine and I could do this; apprehension and worry whispered uneasy thoughts about what might happen. My faith allowed me to believe everything would be okay, although I felt curious and uncertain as to how it would all play out.

Planning for my return to school had begun in August of 2003, just two months after my accident. Every part of my rehabilitation, both physical and cognitive, had been building to this point. Coach Att had begun coming to Scottish Rite in October to help me academically and to help my therapists understand me better. Misunderstandings created by not knowing me as an individual had been causing problems for everybody. Coach Att helped bridge that gap.

By Christmas I had felt I would be ready to return after graduating from day rehab at Scottish Rite. Mom and Dad had stayed in contact with school personnel, giving them almost play-by-play updates on my academic and physical recovery. As the end of day rehab had approached, my parents, Coach Att, and other representatives from the school met with the staff at Scottish Rite to develop the best plan for me. The only thing I kept telling Mom was, "I am *not* going in a wheelchair!" I had insisted that I was ready to walk using my "Papa Walker" and I could make it with no problems.

***

DAVID "ATT" STEPHENSON: I was really amazed at how smoothly Eric transitioned back to school. I know he had a very strong support group: his family, friends, and, of course, the faculty and staff of Commerce High School. Everyone loved Eric. He was so friendly and thoughtful of others. At first, he struggled with his schoolwork, but he showed rapid improvement. He was such a hard worker and wanted to learn, or relearn, as was the case in many ways.

***

HANK TILLER: I was so excited that Radio was finally going to be able to come back to school and hang out like old times. It was going to be a tough road, but I knew he would be up for the challenge. I also knew that he had a great group of friends who were behind him 100 percent and would help him or push him when things got rough.

***

Sunday, March 7. I wanted to be reoriented before I started back. So, Mom and Dad drove me to the school and let me walk around with my walker to get used to the place again. The school didn't have a large campus or a lot of steps. It wasn't too difficult to get around, but I certainly now saw the halls, classrooms, and walkways from a new and very different perspective.

My first schedule had only one class. After a week of attending school, a special committee would discuss my goals and plans and create a playbook for me. A few years ago, Commerce High had converted to a ninety-minute block schedule with four classes per day. My schedule allowed me to go to Athens for physical therapy in the mornings and be back at school by 1:00 p.m. for my class. This way I could spend time with my friends at lunch and then go to fourth block. I decided to start with a class and a teacher I liked—US history with Coach Jarvis. Now I could talk about the Civil War without annoying him, and he couldn't make me do jumping jacks in class!

My injuries classified me as OHI (other health impairment), specifically a traumatic brain injury. That was a good thing because it gave me the support of the special education department. They could provide help to make me successful in the classroom, but I would still be expected to complete all the work required for graduation. For one thing, they said I could be in school until I turned twenty-two to graduate, if need be. No way! My goal was to graduate with my class, so extra time was one thing I didn't need. The special education department's biggest and best support was hiring Wes Massey, a paraprofessional assigned to help me at school. Wes, a former Commerce athlete, was in college studying to be a teacher. He was a senior on our 2000 state championship football team. We became good friends as he helped me go from lunch to class, take notes, and study for tests, plus all sorts of things he wasn't required to do. He drove an old, ugly minivan that I called his "pimp-mobile." Like a great utility player, if something was needed, Wes did his best to make it happen. He became invaluable over the next year and a half in helping me reach my ultimate goal—to graduate with a college preparatory diploma and to walk at graduation with my friends as the class of 2005.

March 15, 2004. Individual education plan. The IEP committee met to discuss my progress during my first week back at school. This group included teachers, school administrators, special education director Dr. Susan Galis, Wes, my parents, and me. I was a little uneasy and didn't say much at first. This was a rare experience for a student—meeting with a lot of top school authorities when you're not even in trouble. Both Coach Jarvis and Wes commented on how focused I'd been and how driven I was to succeed. Coach Jarvis even said that my desire to graduate with my class might be making me a better student and more focused on academics than I was before.

One issue was whether I was ready to add another class. I felt that I was ready and voiced my opinion that I could handle it. We decided to add a math and money management class with Mrs. Blair to my schedule and have me start coming to school earlier. Now I'd be at school for third block to take the math class before lunch and US history afterward.

Another decision to be made at this meeting was whether I should take the Georgia High School Graduation Test, which would be given the next week. That four-day test was a real pain in the neck for normal, healthy students, so the committee had to decide whether I was able to take it. Each part of the test—

language arts, social studies, math, and science—would be given on a separate day. Even worse was a writing test that I would have to take during the summer. Committee members were concerned about both my cognitive ability to pass it and my physical stamina to take a test that could last up to three hours per day. The good thing was that Wes could help me stay focused by reading the questions to me and allowing me to respond. After much discussion, they agreed to let me try it, basically figuring, "What's the worst thing that could happen?" If I failed or if I didn't take it, I'd have to retake it. If I somehow passed, I'd be done with it. I kept remembering Philippians 4:13 and planned to show them that I could do this.

Survival. Wes and I both survived the whole week of testing and waiting for the results. To pass each test, I had to earn a score of 500. I actually passed math with a 501 and almost passed social studies with a 496. That was one down and three to go. This boosted my confidence and morale.

My dreams, and those of my family, were coming true. I was back at school and continuing my physical and speech therapies. My physical therapy was designed to help me become more independent at school and at home. My primary goals, of course, were to get my diploma with my class and to walk without a cane or walker. In speech we worked on volume control, word retrieval, and auditory memory—keeping Radio's "sound system" switched on and fine-tuned was very important! All these skills would help me in the classroom and in my overall recovery.

Friends. From the moment I came back to school, I clearly understood how important my friends were to my life and especially to my making it through school. They seemed to be more excited than I was about my return to school and were very determined to help me succeed. John 15:13 says, "Greater love has no one than this, that he lay down his life for his friends" (BSB). Every day my friends gave up some of their time to help me get to classes or the cafeteria, study for a test, carry my book bag, or do something else they thought I needed. They even got my lunch for me and helped me take notes. They pushed me to improve every day and to get the best out of myself. They wouldn't let me give up now even if I wanted to quit. They wanted me to graduate with them as much as I did. My teachers took extra time to help me learn the material and to make sure I understood everything. Needing so much help was frustrating and embarrassing, but I'm glad and blessed to have had so many people who were willing to help me. Mom kept telling me that it was going to be a long, tough road. I kept asking her if she really believed I could make it, because I sure did.

Another IEP meeting. At the end of March, we held another meeting to decide my immediate and long-term future. First of all, we figured out which credits I'd earned, what else I needed for graduation, and how to earn them in the time I had left. I needed twenty-eight credits to graduate. I had earned sixteen my first two years, and had twelve to go. Commerce's block schedule gave me an advantage. Between the classes I was taking and some I could take during the summer, it was possible to get back on track to graduate on time! This would take a lot of work from me, my family, friends, and teachers, but it could be done and I fully intended to do it.

A rigorous academic regimen. I could finish out the year in the two classes I was taking and complete the first part of each course during the summer. That would earn me two credits toward graduation. In addition, my physical therapy could be counted as weight training and physical education credits, giving me two more. Finally, my speeches and journals from speech therapy were allowed to count as language arts assignments for two more—a total of six credits. Between my efforts and the school system's help, I was actually getting caught up!

Hardworking tutors. Mom and Dad often commented that they were working harder and studying more to help me than they ever did when they were students in high school. Since Erin took most of these courses a couple of years ago, she helped a lot. Like our parents, she claimed it was harder preparing me to pass the classes than it ever was to ace them herself as a student. My friends were also dedicated, enthusiastic tutors.

The grind. Earning a diploma is hard work. Every night, Erin, my parents, and/or friends worked with me for hours. They quizzed me over and over to make sure I remembered and understood everything. This is especially true of Erin. When I asked her to give me a break, she told me I had to keep testing myself to make sure I was growing and improving. She is tougher than Coach Savage or any coach I ever had or want to have.

On May 19, 2004, we had another IEP meeting. We discussed my progress and made plans for the future. One of the biggest questions was whether to continue toward a college preparatory diploma or switch to a technical diploma. The big difference between the two was that the technical diploma didn't require as much math or any foreign language. Most of my teachers strongly suggested (pushed!) switching because I would be able to take more electives and the work wouldn't be as hard or stressful. I understood their good intentions and what they were saying, but I wanted to continue on the college prep track and prove to everyone that Philippians 4:13 isn't a lie. I really could "do everything through Christ who strengthens me." As the meeting went on, it looked like the decision had already been made and I would be switched. Time out! That was not acceptable!

For the first time in one of these meetings, I interrupted the proceedings to speak up for myself. I made it quite clear to everybody that I wanted to remain on the college preparatory–diploma track. I was shaking, but I had to make sure they knew how strongly I felt about this. Finally I pleaded, "I can do this. Give me a chance."

Those few words changed the meeting's tone abruptly and made some eyes a bit misty. It felt good to stand up for myself and to know that others were beginning to believe in me, too. Dr. Galis smiled at me and asked, "With an attitude like that, how can we not let him try?" Touchdown!

***

DR. SUSAN GALIS-WHITE, director of special education services, Commerce City Schools: This was one of many emotional meetings we held to make decisions regarding Eric's educational future. One of the main reasons the meetings were emotional was that participants cared deeply for Eric and wanted him to have every opportunity to be successful. Decisions were not right or wrong or black and white. We made decisions at each crossroad with a great deal of discussion and effort to ensure that Eric could achieve the best outcome possible. At times, there was a great deal of disagreement regarding educational decisions.

This particular meeting was a turning point that we couldn't know was significant until we could look back much later. Eric's active participation in this meeting changed the outcome. He let us know that we needed to listen to his desires. Eric then proceeded to prove that he could indeed graduate with a college prep diploma!

***

GREG JARVIS: This meeting was very emotional for me. I was one of Radio's biggest supporters, but I felt that he should consider switching over to the technical track for graduation. It was emotional to see Radio stand up for himself and to realize that I was placing limits on him without intending to. Who was I to do that? Some kind of expert? Thank God Radio spoke up and Dr. Galis listened to him. This is one of the most pivotal moments in my life and career, and I go back to it when working with students today.

***

ANGIE REDMON: The school was wonderful to work with. They listened to us and did everything they could to prepare for Eric's return. The only real disagreement was over the graduation track. I knew that some of his teachers were trying to make it easier for him and had his best interests at heart, but I was really proud of him when he said, "Give me a chance." They listened to him and gave him that chance.

***

Once that issue was settled, I made sure everyone knew my next goal was to graduate with my friends. Even though I understood that I had until the age of twenty-two to graduate, my plan was to be ready to march in with those who had started school with me in kindergarten. I was already missing football, golf, and wrestling with my friends, and I didn't intend to miss graduating with them!

A tough gig. Once my schedule was worked out for the summer of 2004, I realized it was going to keep me and a lot of others extremely busy. This academic regimen was a lot rougher than my summer 2003 physical regimen. In football, we would call it "piling on." This time the danger was brain strain rather than physical strain.

First of all, I had to make up the first nine weeks of the courses in US history and math and money management to get those credits. The foreign language credit would come from taking a Spanish course online with the understanding that I'd take the final exam at school with Señora Ward, our Spanish teacher. In addition, I had to make up my junior American literature class, which required a lot of reading—never my favorite activity! Coach Jarvis came through for me with recordings of the required books so I could hear and read the words at the same time. This was the academic equivalent of having big, fast offensive linemen when you're the quarterback. Mr. Miller, my language arts teacher, worked with me on grammar, another painful requirement. Then there were the End of Course Tests in US history and junior American literature. Finally, after finishing the math and money management course, I worked on Algebra II to be prepared for that class my senior year. What a blessing that Walt Massey, Wes's brother, taught math at our school and helped me over that hurdle. To add to that, I still had to retake the Georgia High School Graduation Tests in language arts, social studies, science, and writing. If I hadn't already had a TBI, this level of academic "piling on" could create one!

I worked as hard that summer as I'd ever worked. Before the wreck, I had been content being an average student and not being particularly motivated to excel academically. To tell the truth, my major academic goals at that time were staying eligible for sports at school and out of trouble at home. Now, I had to study a lot harder just to pass a course. Not only did I have to work hard, my entire family had to work along with me, as did many of my friends and teachers. I am so grateful to them for giving up countless hours of their time to help me study and to drill and quiz me as often as needed. All the time and effort they spent to help me succeed will never be forgotten. They were true friends as the Bible describes friends, "laying down their lives" for me by giving me their time.

To say that the summer was a grueling academic marathon is an understatement. I had six hours of classes every day! I couldn't do it without everyone who helped me. Teachers came every day, spending hours of their summer vacation time with me. Erin tutored me in every free moment she had. Mom and Dad studied with me and drilled me constantly with study guide questions and reviews. To pass my junior language arts course, I had to read four books and write three papers in addition to passing the grammar part. Piled on top of the academics was my physical therapy schedule. My goal was not only to graduate with my friends, but to walk with them as well, so PT was vital.

The best news of the summer: I passed the language arts and writing sections of the graduation test! Now I'd completed everything I needed to get back on track and begin my senior year with a chance to graduate on time.

***

ERIN REDMON MOORE: It was so, so frustrating, for us and him. School was always so easy for me, and not so easy for Eric. And then you add in the brain injury and the short-term memory problems, and everything was just harder for him. But what I also remember was his sense of humor and ability to laugh at himself through it all. And that rings true for dealing with all aspects of his injury even now. Eric's positive attitude helped him survive, got him through school, and continues to push him through every day.

***

Nothing ventured, nothing gained. Our family, friends, and doctors continued to research new therapies. To help in my physical recovery, my parents and I decided to go to Houston in July for some experimental impulse treatments.

Vacation. Before the Houston trip, my family enjoyed something we missed last year. We went to the beach in Destin, Florida, and I had a ball. This was a trip that several family members made every year, and it was good to be able to go with them. Warm sand and ocean waves beat the heck out of hospital rooms and rehab facilities! When you consider the girls on the beach, the view is much better, too. Catching a barracuda on our deep-sea fishing trip was super exciting! They don't describe it as "wrestling with a big fish" for nothing. To make it better, I could now pronounce "barracuda" and tell folks all about it.

On to Houston. In Houston, I received three treatments designed to help my balance and walking. Each treatment took over an hour and left me feeling very tired. In addition to the impulse therapy, the research staff tried a new spray on me. It was proven to improve short-term memory, so I was game. Even though I was their first traumatic brain injury patient to use it, they were very optimistic about the results. With their treatments and my therapy program, I was definitely improving.

Joe Nichols, live and in person! Back at home, another great event happened: a Joe Nichols concert. He released the song "The Impossible," which had become an inspiration to me. This seemed like a miracle and a dream come true—my family, friends Tommy and Mary Beth, and I attended his concert and met Joe after the show. I told him how that song inspired me and that I sang it at my graduation from Scottish Rite. He let me see his bus and I promised him I would walk on graduation day. To meet and personally thank him for singing this song and inspiring me was really special.

CHAPTER 9

SENIOR YEAR

For we walk by faith, not by sight.
—2 Corinthians 5:7 (NKJV)

Senior realities. One of the first "regular kid" things I did for my senior year was get senior pictures taken. I'll always be grateful to Coach Savage for allowing me to put on my football uniform one last time and be included in the team picture. Finally I felt like a real senior! The bad thing was realizing and accepting deep down the hard facts that I wouldn't play football my senior year, and I could never play any contact sport again. That hurt more than any hit on the football field. Disappointed and sad about this, I forced myself to make a positive decision—if I couldn't play with them, I could be their biggest cheerleader on the sidelines.

Friends, tried and true. I can't stress enough how important my friends are. The first day of school, David Bray called and asked if he could drive me to school. That's role reversal for sure. He's younger than me, and before I had my accident, I drove him to school. I had been on the way to David's birthday party fifteen months prior when my accident happened. He wanted me to ride to school with friends, like everyone else did. Being driven to school by your parents is not for seniors! Mom's friend Susan Hughes picked me up every afternoon after school so Mom could work a full day.

Protection. Since my balance was still a bit unsteady, friends walked with me to classes, serving as blockers and guards to keep me from being jostled in the crowded halls. Others literally picked me up and gave me piggyback rides if we ran late. Their motivation was simple—these guys were not going to let me fail now.

Racking up credits. During fall semester I had three academic courses: algebra II, economics, and senior language arts. The preparation I did for these classes in the summer really helped. My language arts teacher was Ms. Bozeman. She also taught me in middle school, so she knew me better than most teachers. She came to my house during the summer and helped me get ready for the class. My fourth class was a combined class of speech therapy on Mondays and Wednesdays and physical therapy on Tuesdays and Thursdays. On Fridays I would go home and rest before the football game. I'm living proof that you can take the player out of the football game, but you can't take football out of the player!

Ups and downs. My strengths were my attitude and drive to succeed. There were still several weaknesses to overcome, including my treacherous short-term memory, short attention span, unsteady balance, and the danger of getting overtired. As in the past, I could be easily distracted at times, but Ritalin helped me to remain focused. To cope with these issues, my teachers gave me tests more often so I would have less information to recall and less time to forget. I wrote everything down in a calendar, a skill I learned somewhat unwillingly at Scottish Rite. Even though I took notes in class, my teachers gave me copies of their notes to make sure I had everything I needed. They also gave me a little longer to complete assignments so I didn't have to rush. Coach Jarvis's testing strategy from the previous year really helped. He let me finish one page of a test and then take a minute to review my notes before getting the next page. As he graded the test, I reviewed my notes again. Then he let me correct my wrong answers for partial credit. This repetition really helped to stick the material in my memory so when I took the End of Course Tests, I was able to remember more of the information. One of my proudest moments was passing his US history test on my first attempt without having to correct it, proving the truth of my early protests: "I'm not stupid!"

Of all of my classes, my biggest problem was algebra II. I understood the material, but any time I had a test or had to turn in an assignment, I couldn't get the answers on the paper correctly. I would do a problem correctly, and then fifteen minutes later I couldn't remember how I did it. My teacher, Mr. Bagwell, had concerns that I didn't understand the math and wondered whether I could pass the course. Both of us were frustrated and really didn't know what to do. Mr. Bagwell was highly respected as a teacher, and his son, Adam, was in my youth group. He had overcome vision problems to be a great teacher and wanted me to succeed as much as I did. My problem was finding a way to prove to him that I could do it.

Coach Jarvis left Commerce High to teach and coach at Mill Creek High School with his brother. This upset me, but he still lived near me and kept in touch weekly. A lot of times he came over on Sunday nights when Ben Wilson was tutoring me in math. Ben was one of the smartest people in our school as well as a great offensive lineman and wrestler. He was also the player who had broken my collarbone (clavicle, per the doctor!) years ago in youth football. Ben couldn't fix my collarbone back then, but he saw that math was causing me more pain than the broken clavicle ever did. True friend that he was, he did his best to ease my academic pain by tutoring me in math.

One fateful night, Mom expressed our concerns about the math class to Coach Jarvis. My graduation wouldn't happen without those math credits. I explained my difficulty putting the answers down correctly when I had to write them out. Coach Jarvis knew that I understood the math because he had seen and heard me explaining problems to Ben during our tutoring sessions. Like a good coach, he analyzed the situation and devised a new play: if Ben and I went to math class early (it was first period) for extra tutoring, Mr. Bagwell could hear me explain the problems to Ben. This would demonstrate that I understood the material much better than my grades showed. Like the great teacher he is, Mr. Bagwell understood what my problem was and helped me overcome it by trying that strategy. It worked, and I still have a lot of respect for Mr. Bagwell. In the end, I passed all my classes first semester!

Good news. My friends assured me that I was still a member of the class of 2005. I was given a senior superlative: most unforgettable. At the homecoming dance they named me homecoming king. The Thursday Night Crew still came over on Thursday nights, and I still cheered for the Tigers on Friday nights.

Bad news. I failed the social studies and science sections of the graduation test again. I was getting closer to the required scores, but running out of testing opportunities before graduation. I reminded myself, "I can do all things through Christ . . ."

Christmas holidays and the end of the semester. We went back to Houston for a second round of impulse treatments and prayed they would help me improve my balance. This time I knew what to expect, so they were easier to tolerate than they were the summer before.

Christmas in Commerce. It was a big, happy surprise to learn that a Christmas tree would be decorated in my honor for the annual Children's Healthcare of Atlanta "Festival of Trees" fundraiser. "Radio's Tree" was designed, decorated, and displayed at the Georgia World Congress Center! After the show closed, the tree was to be delivered to me. Then a bright idea popped into my head. Before I could forget it, I asked them to display my tree in a Commerce bank so more people could see and enjoy it. If all went the way I hoped, some people might be inspired to make donations to Children's Healthcare. I loved being able to share joy, beauty, and support—giving back to those who had enabled me to rebuild my body and life, and paying it forward for those who needed similar help.

The crunch was on. As the second semester began, I had a new set of classes and no margin for error. I had to pass them all in order to graduate. My classes were advanced algebra/trigonometry, human anatomy, and political systems, as well as Spanish II with Señora Ward. This was my first Spanish class with my friends; all the others were online classes I had taken during the summer. And, just like the summer, it was a lot of hard work. One friend, Marco Zelaya, really helped me, so it was not too bad. I will admit that when you're still struggling to relearn English, learning Spanish feels like piling on for sure.

Good news in January. I passed the social studies section of the graduation test! I got all twelve questions correct in the information-processing skills part of the test, and eleven out of twelve in the map skills section. Doing well in these areas proved that I could think and figure things out again. Hallelujah! I was also going to as many wrestling matches as possible.

A successful spring semester with just one more big hurdle. I was doing well in all my classes, getting excited about graduating, but still feeling apprehensive about the science graduation test. My prayer was that taking a science class that semester would boost my chances to pass this monster.

March. I felt very nervous about taking the science test—this was my last chance to pass it before graduation. If I failed this time, all I could hope to receive at graduation was a certificate of attendance. I could walk with my friends at the ceremony, but I wouldn't get a diploma. Although they would allow me to come back after graduation, take the test again, and get my diploma, it just wasn't the same. My goal was to actually graduate with my class—no faking! Waiting on the results seemed to take forever. This kind of pressure can shake even a strong faith a little bit, but I wasn't hitting the panic button.

April and May seemed to fly by, crammed full of activities, challenges, and victories.

Not my dream spring break. I went back to Houston for more treatments instead of partying at the beach with my friends. This time I traveled without a wheelchair. I just had my "Papa Walker," and I didn't need anything else.

Senior prom. Dancing without my wheelchair was a lot more fun than dancing in it. Yes, it had been an asset doing "The Tootsie Roll" at the homecoming dance, but there were definite disadvantages, too.

Speaking engagements. The Fellowship of Christian Athletes invited me to speak and give my testimony at a fundraising banquet. Their primary speaker was Clemson's football coach, Tommy Bowden, giving me a chance to thank him for his Valentine's Day phone call during that dark time at Scottish Rite. I also spoke at Commerce High School's Fellowship of Christian Athletes meeting and at several churches, sharing with everyone how much my faith and their prayers, help, and friendship meant to me.

"Mr. Football." At the athletic sports banquet in May, the cheerleaders named me "Mr. Football." Those girls were really special! Then Coach Savage presented my framed number-thirty-seven football jersey and announced it would hang in the Commerce field house weight room as a symbol of hard work and determination. It was hard—really hard!—not to choke up as memories flooded in. I'd come a long way from running around on the field in my cousin's helmet, carrying the water bucket, misplacing the kicking tee, blowing a chance to score by showing off, saving a game and my chicken wings with an interception and touchdown, celebrating my birthdays at cheerleading competitions . . . and so many other experiences with these friends. At last I fully understood the importance of teamwork and why my Commerce jersey still didn't have my name on the back!

The suspense was over. About a week before graduation, the news came—I PASSED THE SCIENCE TEST! I needed a score of 500 and scored a 512. In addition, I scored 83 percent in the processing-skills section, and the state average was 77. I wasn't stupid! My mind still worked. Slower, perhaps, but it worked.

Thank you, Dr. Galis and the IEP committee, for listening to my plea and giving me a chance. Now I just had to finish all the academic work and earn passing grades in all my classes to meet another "impossible" goal. Although I would have to use my faithful "Papa Walker," I could graduate with a real college preparatory diploma and walk with my classmates to receive our long-anticipated diplomas. No sweat! I knew I could do this. I believed I was living proof of an old saying that says, "God turns impossible into I'm possible."

May 20, 2005, was a special day for many reasons. The fact that I was walking and graduating with my friends was an obvious reason, but not the only one. It showed what can happen when you truly believe and live Philippians 4:13—you can do all things through Christ. It also demonstrated the truth of John 15:13 and what happens when true friends give of themselves to help a friend in need. This special day showed what a powerful force God is in my life; my friends showed everyone just how loving and supportive they actually are; my family celebrated our victories over my challenges; and I provided living proof that prayers work.

Honoring our traditions. Being a small school in a small town, Commerce High has many long-standing traditions. Whether it's running down the hill to play football on Friday night, going to the local truck stop after a game, or cruising around the railroad tracks on Saturday night, these traditions are passed down like rites of passage. One special tradition is the way caps are thrown at graduation. When all the graduates have been announced and have received their diplomas, they march together to the end zone. Once everyone is there, they throw their caps into the air together for their last official act as Commerce High School students. I couldn't wait to throw mine.

Oh no—rain! This potential spoiler created a stunning display of loyalty and caring at the end of our graduation program. We were actually getting our diplomas when it began to drizzle, not too heavy, but enough to be uncomfortable. Mr. Drew, our principal, began calling our names faster, trying to complete the ceremony before the weather got worse. My last name begins with R, and it was taking him a little while to get there even though he was going as fast as he could. The drizzle wet the grass more by the minute and doubt whispered to me, *Even though Wes is walking beside me and I have my walker, can I keep my balance on such a slippery surface? What if I slip and fall? Falling can injure a lot more than my dignity. Have I worked this hard and gotten this far just to spoil graduation for everyone?*

My big moment arrived. I was so focused that I didn't hear a sound in the stadium as I stood up, walked to the podium with my trusty "Papa Walker," and received my diploma. Meeting this goal and graduating with my friends was a bigger thrill than making a game-saving interception in the fourth quarter! After I received my diploma, I noticed the ovation from the crowd for me, and I thought they were as happy as I was. Now I just had to wait for Mr. Drew to get through the rest of the names, and I could participate in our traditional grand finale.

The ceremony was over. As we marched out to throw our caps, I noticed that the rain had stopped. The football field was pretty wet, and keeping my balance on wet grass was always tough. Walking as fast as I could just wasn't fast enough to keep up with the others. Would they wait on me to get there or go on without me?

Friendship triumphed. As soon as the Thursday Night Crew realized what was happening, they came to my rescue. Hank and Caleb came back to get me, picked me up, put me on their shoulders, and carried me to the end zone like a conquering hero. The rain from the sky had stopped, but tears were raining down the faces of the audience. This was neither my plan nor the most proper and dignified way to march at graduation, but it worked. With a grateful heart and the rest of the Commerce High School class of 2005, I threw my cap as high as I could. Watching it rise into the night, my faith rose to new heights. As our caps fell to the ground, the doubts, fears, and frustrations of the past twenty-three months fell away. With God's help and the support of family and friends, I was alive and achieving "The Impossible"!

***

CALEB JORDAN: It was as big a moment for us as it was for Radio. He was so much a part of everything we did in high school, and we wanted to make sure he knew it. We couldn't throw our caps without him.

***

My life will never be the way it was before the accident, but I graduated from high school and into a stronger faith, a deeper understanding, and a greater appreciation for the love and goodness of God, family, friends, and Commerce, Georgia.

***

BOBBY REDMON: When Eric walked across that stage to receive his diploma, I knew he would be okay. Any person with that amount of drive, determination, and ability to impact an entire community could achieve anything.

***

ANGIE REDMON: As Eric graduated, I couldn't help but think how good God is. When everyone began cheering for him and I could feel the love of the community, it was overwhelming. It started to rain near the end of the ceremony, making it hard for him to walk. When his buddies came back to pick him up and carry him to throw his cap, it was almost symbolic of how the entire community had lifted him up throughout the journey.

***

ERIN REDMON MOORE: At graduation, I was worried about Eric walking and making it through the ceremony. Of course, he did fine, but I worried all the way until his friends raised him up on their shoulders and carried him off the field. When I couldn't worry anymore about his falling, I just remember how very proud I was and how very much he deserved this time of triumph. He had accomplished more in the last two years than anyone else on the field, more even than most of them would accomplish in a lifetime. I was just so proud of him.

***

DAVID "ATT" STEPHENSON: When Eric graduated, I was so proud of him. I had my doubts in the early going if he would make it and graduate. He had come a long way, and I knew that he had worked a lot harder than most of the graduates. He was so determined and had such great support from his family and friends. They really pushed him to succeed.

***

HANK TILLER: Our graduation had to be one of the shortest in the history of all high school graduations because it started raining! It was very emotional because Radio was able to use his walker and march with the rest of our graduating class. When we were all done getting wet and waiting to throw our caps, we realized Radio was having a difficult time walking. We ran over to him, picked him up, and carried him to join the rest of the class so we could throw our caps together. There was no way we were going to throw our caps without him! Then we went back to his house for our graduation party, and I can't talk about the rest—that's just for us to know about!

CHAPTER 10

LIFE'S A PARTY

I have come that they may have life, and that
they may have it more abundantly.
—John 10:10 (NKJV)

2005 to 2015. Since graduating from high school, I spend most of my time doing three things: (1) continuing my rehabilitation, (2) sharing my testimony, and (3) starting my businesses. To be honest, in the first months after graduation I had no idea what I should do now or in the future. Most of my friends were going off to college. That wasn't a practical plan for me because I was still learning to walk and working on other "after the accident" issues. I decided to remain at home and increase my physical therapy until I could walk without a walker or cane. As I told Mom, I felt I had to do it while I was young and she shouldn't worry about my future. I knew God would lead me, but it was frustrating not to be sure about His purpose for my life. It's hard to plan your route before you know your destination!

Financial independence. With college out of the playbook, I decided to use some money from my graduation gifts to start a business. I bought a couple of vending machines, loaded them with drinks and snacks, and put them in Uncle Tommy's gyms. This operation is small by most standards, but it's easy, enjoyable, profitable, and something productive to do. At least once each week I restock the machines and empty the money boxes. I'm not becoming a millionaire, but I'm doing okay moneywise. The goal of carrying my own weight financially is becoming as important to me as carrying my physical weight had been at Scottish Rite.

Left behind. Frustration still dogged me after graduation. It was hard to stay at home and watch my friends leave Commerce and go away to college. Actually feeling left behind in so many areas was extra hard this time because the Thursday Night Crew wasn't there to pick me up and carry me with them. It wasn't their fault; they were just pursuing their dreams and goals, which were now far different from mine. They still visited me as often as they could, and it was obvious that leaving me behind after being together since kindergarten made their hearts heavy. Mine would get heavy, too, realizing they were achieving grown-up goals while I was stuck relearning how to walk.

Church troubles. To make it worse, the feeling that I had been left behind also tackled me at church. Most of my Sunday school classmates were gone, and I was now too old for the youth group. I spent a lot of time in prayer, talking to God, and seeking His guidance to find my path and my purpose.

Even with a foggy view of my future, faith and perhaps a little pride prompted me to assure Mom, "God is always there whenever I need Him." Sure enough, it wasn't too long before He guided me into a new church and a new business venture that combined my faith, my outlook on life, and my desire to tell my story to help and encourage others.

Sharing my testimony is my favorite thing to do because it allows me to show the power of God to others and to prove that He is still actively involved in the lives of those who look to Him. Every time He allows me to speak, He opens more doors for me—even when I can't see any doors ahead.

When Coach Jarvis moved from coaching at Commerce High to Mill Creek, he invited me to speak to various groups at his new school and allowed me to share my story with people I wouldn't have otherwise met. As a matter of fact, the morning after my graduation, while many of my friends were leaving on senior trips, I shared my story with the first senior class at Mill Creek. When he told me he was getting married, I got really scared that he wouldn't have time for me anymore and we would never get my book written. Not so! Coach Jarvis asked me to offer the closing prayer at his wedding, and I accepted. This set in motion another life-changing experience for me. To thank me, he gave me Kyle Maynard's book, *No Excuses.*

Unstoppable. Although Kyle Maynard was born without arms or legs, he refused to let that stop him from doing anything he wanted to do, including participating in sports. Kyle played football in a youth league and eventually became an outstanding wrestler at Collins Hill High School where competition for team positions is huge. Before Mill Creek opened, Collins Hill was Georgia's largest high school and is now the second largest. Kyle was a very small wrestler on a very large mat!

Book therapy. I couldn't put down *No Excuses.* When I finished reading it, I just started over and read it again—a most unusual response for this lifelong reluctant reader. Rereading Kyle's book so many times improved my reading speed and comprehension skills dramatically. I really wanted to meet Kyle, and the opportunity finally came at the Collins Hill wrestling banquet in 2006. Coach Jarvis contacted their wrestling coach, and they arranged for us to meet. When my story and my meeting with Kyle made it to the parents at Collins Hill, some of them began contacting me on my website. Among other things, they told me they were praying for me and encouraged me to keep working to build the kind of life I wanted. This was excellent medicine for me. A good role model and a lot of encouragement are priceless aids to success.

Life goes on. During these first three years after graduation, I made time to push myself as hard as I could to walk again. I went to physical therapy in Athens three days each week and finished my impulse treatments in Houston.

2006. Rebuilding Radio wasn't easy. Although I kept up my redneck therapy regimen as well as the formal therapies, spasticity was a continuing problem, requiring more than standard therapies. Doctors surgically implanted an intrathecal baclofen pump (try spelling or pronouncing that one quickly even without a TBI!) in my abdomen to release medicine directly into my spinal cord. This gave me more control over my muscles. I also went to an outpatient facility operated by Scottish Rite for speech therapy, occupational therapy for my left hand, and Botox injections to help with muscle control.

God's plan. Meanwhile, God continued working out His plan for me. The fiancé of my new physical therapist at Scottish Rite was a youth minister. After she told him about me, he invited me to speak to several different groups. Ironically, I was too busy trying to figure out my life's purpose to realize that God was already using me to fulfill it. Not until I looked back much later did I begin to recognize the patterns of His plan for me. Once again I learned the lesson "Let go and let God."

I'm still a Commerce Tiger. To remain involved in Tiger football, I helped Dad film their games. Before my injuries, watching game films was an integral part of improving my skills, correcting my mistakes, and preparing for upcoming games. In those first disastrous days after the accident, watching their game films let me feel like I was still a part of the team, and that meant a lot to me. I was now climbing up to the press box instead of running down the hill, but I was still a part of the Tiger football team. People were amazed to see me climbing the steps and the ladder to the top of the press box. Not me—it wasn't amazing at all because I knew "I can do all things through Christ . . ."

Wrestling. Going to Tiger wrestling matches isn't such a happy story. I tried attending them, too, but it just wasn't the same after most of my friends graduated. Maybe not having personal relationships with the wrestlers was weakening its appeal for me, or maybe it was because I was too busy with other things.

2007. A lot of things were happening, most of them good, but there was sadness, too. Losing my dog Rudy, who passed away, hurt a lot. He left many great memories, but he took a big piece of my heart with him. Rudy was one of my best friends and most faithful supporters. We always enjoyed each other's company. His warm, sloppy licks comforted me beyond measure in the bad times and amped up my celebrations when good things happened.

The fun side. I began getting exciting opportunities to repay and pass on some of the generosity we had received. Every year since 2003 I'd been helping

Atlanta's Star 94 radio station with their annual radio-thon for Children's Healthcare of Atlanta. Their radio-thon and the celebrities who visited me during a very discouraging period when I was a patient at Scottish Rite meant more to me than I can say. I also started helping to raise money for the Ronald McDonald House in Dunwoody. The camaraderie at "our" Ronald McDonald House in Atlanta kept the fire of hope and the light of humor burning brightly during the tough times of day rehab and our growing realization that many of our challenges would never go away. I love paying it forward. Even though I can't see the big picture yet, God is using me, putting me in positions to help people, which is something I truly want to do.

2008. Life's A Party, a new venture. On the fifth anniversary of my accident, my mom and I began a new business: renting equipment for parties. This was Dad's idea, but I believe God inspired Dad and led us in setting it up.

Confirmation. My first order confirmed my belief that this business is God's plan for me. I hadn't even received my equipment when a small church in Ila, Georgia, ordered a tent for their homecoming celebration. I didn't know anyone in Ila, a town about ten miles from Commerce, and had no idea how they knew about me, my business, or how to contact me. Anyway, I accepted the job and made a phone call to set up a rush shipment on the tent I just bought. It seemed miraculous—the tent came in on time, we delivered it to the church, and Life's A Party was officially in business. Later I found out that they called me because their church had been praying for me since my accident.

Success on multiple fronts. Life's A Party was very successful in opening a way for me to do what I love most—meet new people and share my faith. I rented tables, chairs, tents, and other traditional party items as well as inflatables. My inventory included large wet and dry slides, an obstacle course, a castle bounce house, and a large slip-n-slide. This business kept me busy and provided many opportunities to be God's witness and to testify about my life and healing.

Prayers from strangers. Often we rented to someone who had heard my story, but didn't know me personally. Asking me how I was doing provided an opportunity to talk about my faith and God's intervention in my life. Many of them mentioned praying for me after the accident. I'm always touched when people who don't know me tell me they prayed for me. Now they could see what their prayers had accomplished and know that Mom's slogan was right on target: "Prayers work."

People say that God works in mysterious ways. It may seem mysterious to some folks, but I believe that everything is a part of God's plan whether we recognize it or not. Sometimes we just have to do what it says in Corinthians and "live by faith, not by sight."

People ask me all the time where my company's name came from. Looking back a bit, we actually spent a lot of time and thought trying to find a name before coming up with one that really seemed to fit. One idea to tie it into the community was "Tiger Party Rentals," but that just didn't sound quite right. For one thing, it could've driven away some business—we didn't think anyone from Jefferson would ever use our company with that name because they are as proud of their Dragons as Commerce is of our Tigers. We also talked about "Radio's Rentals," but that didn't hit the right notes either. The more I prayed about it, the more two Bible verses kept coming to me: (1) "I've come that they may have life, and have it abundantly" (John 10:10, NKJV). To me, this means we should rejoice and celebrate (i.e., party) every day because Jesus came to give us full, high-spirited lives. (2) "Rejoice always, pray without ceasing, in everything give thanks; for this is the will of God in Christ Jesus for you" (1 Thessalonians 5:16–18, NKJV). Jesus is the reason that life should be a party! I truly believe that the Christian life should be celebrated. All of this led to how we finally got the name.

Helpers. As with everything else in my recovery and rehabilitation, it took many people to help me with my business. Although Mom no longer worked at Baker & Taylor, she still did a lot of work for Uncle Tommy, and she was also my appointments secretary, bookkeeper, and cheerleader. In addition to his construction job, Dad drove my truck, delivered for me, and continued to push me to do more than I thought I can do. When he wasn't available, Kyle Moore, Erin's boyfriend, covered the gap.

Rebuilding Radio continued. To improve my gait, more surgery and rehab were needed. Doctors lengthened the Achilles tendons in my left foot and the toe tendons in my right foot. Sometimes I thought my body was getting more revisions than an old playbook in a new season!

Aging. I'd "outgrown" my eligibility to work with Scottish Rite. To put it bluntly, I'd gotten too old to work with a children's hospital. As a legal adult, this Radio had to change his "minor" station and move to an adult facility. After five years of working together, it was tough to leave the Scottish Rite doctors and staff, but it turned out to be a good thing.

Makeovers. Like going from Grady to Scottish Rite in 2003, my R & R (rebuilding and recovering) changed markedly when I began seeing the staff at the Shepherd Center. These doctors are experts at dealing with adults and are on the cutting edge of new research and techniques. They did more surgery on both my Achilles tendons to help me walk better and put me through another round of rehab. They also operated on my gums because the medicines I'd taken over the years caused severe deterioration. Yep—another top-to-toe makeover!

New fellow travelers. At Shepherd I met a lot of other young people who had various kinds of TBIs. Some were in accidents and others had strokes. Recalling my own fears and frustrations, I enjoyed meeting them and welcomed opportunities to encourage them as much as I could. Like my old friends at the Ronald McDonald House, we shared a common bond that allowed us to share our strengths and help each other deal effectively with similar problems.

A sad ending. December of 2008 ended sadly with the death of one of my best and oldest friends, my grandmother, Nanny Syble. We shared a love of history, football, and the mysteries of the JFK assassination. She was a great storyteller. I listened to her for hours as she brought stories to life. Nanny was likely the one responsible for my love of history. I missed her now and always would, but I knew I'd see her again in Heaven.

Prayers. Dad prayed with me a lot during this period. We knew that God had a purpose and a plan for me, but I was having a hard time seeing them. This really bothered me, so we asked God for signs, for Him to lead us, and for peace as we moved forward. Within a few months several things happened to show me what my purpose was.

First of all, I'd been asked to talk to accident victims and their family members a lot and I could feel God helping me to help them. I'd been asked to speak at churches, high schools, and even some colleges. Being put in all these places to share my testimony and offer encouragement to others finally opened my eyes and allowed me to see that this was my purpose. The second thing was finding a church that was better able to meet my spiritual needs at this time in my life. As people grow and change, their spiritual needs may change, too, and that's what was happening to me. Mount Olive Baptist Church and its people would always mean the world to me. Their love, prayers, and support literally kept me alive and fighting for recovery in the darkest days of my life, so leaving wasn't a reflection on the church or anyone there. Like me, Mount Olive had grown and changed. My youth minister was no longer there, my friends had gone away to college and jobs, and I needed something different for my spiritual growth. I was blessed that God led me to a new church that provided it. Through its outdoor ministry, a program for people who enjoyed hunting, fishing, and the outdoors in general, Maysville Baptist Church filled those needs.

October 2009. Wedding bells for Erin and Kyle. They had begun dating in high school and continued throughout college—it seemed like they'd been together forever. Kyle had been an important part of the Redmon family for a long time. He is quiet and very much like Dad while Erin is just like Mom, so it must have been a match made in Heaven. I felt honored when Erin displayed her independent thinking—she decided not to have a maid of honor, but instead asked me to stand with her during the ceremony as her "man of honor."

Fall 2010. We took a great trip to Boston. This had been on my bucket list for a long time because I love history. It was exciting to see so many famous sites from the American Revolution and to visit the JFK Library. Attending the football game between Boston College and Clemson was fun, even though Clemson lost by six points.

Politics. I was finally able to get actively involved in politics, another longtime interest. This actually started back in 2009 when Aunt Judy was president of the Georgia Utility Contractors Association. She asked me to share my story and testimony at their annual banquet in Atlanta, but didn't tell me that Karen Handel, Georgia's secretary of state, would be there. This turned out to be another turning point for me, although my active political participation wouldn't begin until 2010.

After Karen Handel heard my talk at the banquet, she wrote me a nice letter and planted the seeds of a special friendship. This led to me becoming one of her supporters and campaigning for her as she ran for governor of Georgia. I really enjoyed making phone calls and helping to raise money for her campaign. If I could see into the future, I'd know this wasn't a one-shot deal. I would go on to help in her campaign again when she ran for the US Senate a few years later, and we've become longtime friends.

***

KAREN HANDEL, congresswoman, sixth district, Georgia: We never know what God's plan is for us. Sometimes we cheer it and sometimes we jeer it. The most uplifting scripture for me is Jeremiah 29:11: "For I know the plans I have for you," declares the Lord, "plans to prosper you and not to harm you, plans to give you hope and a future." Eric is a true inspiration. He may not believe that, but he is. I remember to this day the first time I met him at a Georgia Utility Contractors event. He got on the stage, and with will and determination, gave his testimony and told his story. In addition, he became my instant pal. So, here's to Eric and ALL that God has planned for him in the years ahead. I thank him for helping me to be a better person.

***

2011. Erin passed the bar, became a lawyer, and was now a mother. She and Kyle had a wonderful little boy named Cooper who called me "Ya Ya." I loved the nickname even though I didn't know where or why he came up with that name. Cooper was my little buddy; I loved spending time with him and spoiling him a little— Erin said a lot. When Cooper was born, Erin and Kyle decided to use a cord-blood bank in the hope that those stem cells may one day help my recovery.

2012. I supported Ramon Gilbert for sheriff of Jackson County. I was pretty active in his campaign, introducing him and speaking for him several times. Eventually I became his campaign coordinator for our district.

I supported these candidates because they shared my faith, vision, and strong Christian values. While I was disappointed that both my candidates lost their races, I really enjoyed the experience of being actively involved in their campaigns. Campaigning enables me to meet a lot of new people and to share my story with a broader audience. Two fringe benefits are learning more about how our American political system actually works and learning to accept the fact that not every candidate I like can win an election, even with my enthusiastic help.

2012. The urge to write a book became very strong, and I prayed in earnest for guidance to get it done. I mentioned it to Coach Jarvis many times over the years after the accident because I knew he would help me write it. He had always said to let him know when I wanted to start. As the tenth anniversary of my accident approached, I knew it was time to write the book or forget it. We began in June 2012, and our plan was to have it completed and published by June 12, 2013. We got off to a great start and had over half of it written by Christmas. Our goal seemed to be within our reach. We had no idea that this timetable didn't match God's.

Another tradition. My middle school football coach's son, Adam Stephenson, was now a fireman and a good friend. He was a senior on the 2000 state championship team. He picked me up on Christmas Eve and took me to lunch at a local Chinese restaurant. This tradition started as a tribute to the movie *A Christmas Story* and we have continued it to help kick off the twenty-four-hour marathon on TV each year.

Another setback. If I have gained any real wisdom since my accident, it's that my plans don't matter and won't work if they don't fit into God's plan. The difficult-to-pronounce intrathecal baclofen pump that was surgically placed in my side in 2006 to help control my spasticity was due for a checkup and possible replacement in February of 2013. To determine whether I still needed it, we began turning down the pump, gradually decreasing the amount of medicine being released into my body. The result wasn't what I hoped for. A fall at

Christmas and a big drop in my energy level were convincing evidence that I still needed the pump.

2013. Another hospital stay. Surgery to replace the pump was scheduled at Emory University Hospital. Everything went well, until the stomach flu made its rounds. This bout with the flu wasn't easy, but it was not nearly as bad as my flu episode at Scottish Rite. My recovery from both problems gave me time to help my friend Hank celebrate his wedding in April. He wanted me to be a groomsman, a much more familiar role than "man of honor." I felt honored and excited because our Thursday Night Crew would be there. It had been years since all of us were together at one time, so this would be a reunion for us as well as a celebration of Hank's wedding.

Shot down again. For the bachelor party, we rented a cabin for the weekend in Cherokee, North Carolina. I looked forward to a great time celebrating with my buddies. Dad went with me because I was not totally back to a 100 percent recovery from the pump surgery. This gave us some time together without Mom and Erin and the rare opportunity to talk without waiting for them to take a break.

A literal "downfall." On our way to dinner Saturday night, I slipped and fell on the path. The fall itself wasn't all that hard, but my head hit a landscape boulder, breaking my jaw in two places. Instead of dinner, we went to a local hospital to get it checked out and make sure it was only a broken jaw and not another brain injury. One of "the crew" joked that if I had just told them I needed another chapter for my book, they would've helped me make up something instead of having all this medical drama. These guys never quit teasing!

Surgery was an extremely poor substitute for Hank's bachelor party. The local diagnosis was bad news, making Dad and me drive all night to reach an Athens hospital. Surgery to repair my jaw was scheduled for the first thing Sunday morning. After giving me morphine for pain and knowing that my jaw was broken, a staff member asked me if I'd eaten anything. Groggy from morphine and lack of sleep, I answered, "I ate a biscuit for breakfast." Oops! They immediately cancelled the surgery.

Nobody realized that I had eaten the biscuit the day before! My short-term memory problems plus the morphine confused me about when I ate it. You would think a broken jaw would tell them I couldn't possibly have eaten anything since yesterday, but I guess not. It would also seem logical to check my improbable answer with Dad, but apparently they didn't think about that either.

Surgery was rescheduled for Monday. Like a replay of that awful Scottish Rite "two-week inpatient rehab" that lasted more than a month, things weren't going as planned. I ended up with a plate put in my mouth, my jaw wired shut, and orders to eat only soft food for two to four weeks. Like it or not, I had to keep my mouth shut until the wires were removed. Radio was being turned off again.

Not a lost cause. This accident complicated things, but even though it felt like being seriously behind in the fourth quarter of a hard game, Tigers don't quit. I would be there for Hank on his big day, no ifs, ands, or buts! Still banged up and in a lot of pain, but determined and stubborn as ever, I had surgery on Monday, was released on Wednesday, and made it to Amanda and Hank's rehearsal dinner on Friday. While everybody else enjoyed barbeque, I had a delicious milkshake. To be honest, this was the most pain I'd ever experienced, but I was determined to be there for Hank like he had always been there for me.

The wedding was on Saturday. Hank's fiancé, Amanda, wanted all the groomsmen to be neatly groomed and shaved for the ceremony and pictures. I looked more like Frankenstein's monster than a Southern gentleman, but she didn't throw me out.

Mom was worried about the possibility of my falling during the ceremony or festivities, but history repeated itself. Just like they did at graduation, the Thursday Night Crew took care of me by carrying me and propping me up when I needed help. While I was happy for Hank and Amanda, I was also very disappointed at not being able to talk or celebrate with the Thursday Night Crew. Sometimes I think "frustrated" ought to have been my middle name while God was teaching me to keep my mouth shut!

Back at home. It didn't take long to get sick of milkshakes and seriously aggravated at not being able to work on my book. The predicted two weeks of my mouth being wired shut turned into four weeks, which then turned into eight weeks. Coach Jarvis and I went through pictures for the book one night, but that was all the progress we could make. After praying hard, I decided there must've be a reason for the delays and tried not to worry.

The toughest part was being unable to talk. I wrote Mom a note reminding her that the last time I went this long without talking was when I was in a coma. To add to my misery, I had to go to the doctor every week. I'd lost sixteen pounds, and I was dogged by depression because I couldn't finish my book. Once again, I had to learn who was in control and to "let go and let God."

The wires finally came off the first week in June so I could talk, eat, and finish the draft of the book on June 12. Now we could begin the editing process. Looking back, I believe that God wanted me to include my broken-jaw ordeal to show that I was still struggling after all these years and I had to turn things over to Him when they weren't going the way I wanted them to go. It's not easy, but when I get really frustrated, I go to Him in prayer because the most important lesson I've ever learned is that prayers work!

Major setbacks in the editing process. Our original editor, the high school principal's wife and a friend to our entire community, suddenly passed away just before Christmas. She had planned to begin editing right after the holidays.

Off to a bad start in January 2014. The year had barely begun when a pipe burst and created almost as much damage and disruption in our house as my accident created in my body. Now we had to restore and remodel our whole house—residential R & R! Mom, Dad, and I lived in a hotel for several months while the insurance company and the contractors worked on the details of rebuilding, restoring, or replacing almost everything in our house.

May brought good news. Being an uncle is full of happy surprises. Erin and Kyle were blessed and had a beautiful baby girl. Harper Louise was going to be spoiled by her Uncle Radio, just like Cooper! I wondered if she would call me "Ya Ya," or invent her own name for me? Time would tell, but I was glad to have a niece.

So much had happened since that June day in 2003, but I couldn't complain. Everything happens for a reason, and God continued to take care of me. Once this book was published, life would get back to normal—whatever "normal" was.

CHAPTER 11

MOVING FORWARD

Let your eyes look straight ahead;
fix your gaze directly before you.
—Proverbs 4:25 (NIV)

June 12, 2014. I began to write this a year after my first timetable's publication date! Two surgeries and a broken jaw gave me time to reflect back to eleven years ago today when my life changed in the blink of an eye and the crash of a car. I am human, so I do sometimes wonder what my life would be like had I never been in an accident. Would I have starred in three sports in high school? Gone to college? Attended my favorite school, the University of South Carolina, or gone to Clemson like my sister? Stayed at home and gone to a local junior college? Would I be married? With or without children? Managing the turf and teaching golf and swimming at Deer Trail, or doing something entirely different?

Before this journey of recovery began, I had started thinking about what I wanted to be and do after high school, taking my classes more seriously, and considering studying turf management or engineering. Like almost everyone else in my class, I had my plans and dreams and thought I had it all under control.

Now I realize that I don't have *anything* under control, but God does. God has a bigger and better plan for my life than I could ever imagine. I believe God sent me back here to finish my work on Earth. Jeremiah 29:11 is one of my favorite verses because in it God says, "For I know the plans I have for you, plans to prosper you and not to harm you, plans to give you hope and a future" (NIV). I often ponder the whys and what-ifs and then realize He is using me to fulfill His plans. As long as I'm here on Earth, I have work to do for Him.

I hope and pray that reading my story helps you to realize how precious your life is and how important it is for you to build a relationship with God and to have Jesus Christ as your Lord and Savior. I continue to pray for all the traumatic brain injury survivors and their families who are struggling with life-changing events. My unmet goal is to walk without a walker or any other assistance. I'll continue working on that until I'm successful or the Lord calls me home to Heaven. Either way, one day I'll no longer need my "Papa Walker." I've learned, and sometimes relearned, that "prayers work" and that maintaining a positive attitude, being blessed with wonderful family and friends, and having the right relationship with God makes my life a party. I hope yours is, too.

My friend Hank is now a fireman for Hall County. To show that God is still in charge, his recruiting class is number thirty-seven. Both of us realize the significance of that number—my high school football jersey was thirty-seven. Hank and Amanda had a baby girl in February 2015.

I continue to help the Ronald McDonald House Charity provide a "home away from home" for other families as they had for my family. I held my first fundraising golf tournament to raise more money for this project. When I was in the hospital, a group held a golf tournament for me and named it "Play fore Eric." I decided to use that, and our goal was to raise $10,000, but we topped that. Once again, we saw the hand of God working in our lives. Who would have thought that on a nine-hole golf course in a small town like Commerce we could raise over $12,000? The house was finally completed and opened on December 17, 2015, a wonderful Christmas gift for accident victims, their families, Team Radio, and me. One of the rooms is dedicated to Team Radio, which was born June 12, 2003, to help me survive and recover from my injuries. Now, we're able to help others and remember the blessings that helped us get this far.

Unfortunately, though, there has been sadness, too. My Aunt Brenda was diagnosed with cancer and passed away on October 18, 2015. Mom was sad and I wished I could help, but I really couldn't. One thing that helped was making caramel apples to sell to raise money for the Ronald McDonald House. One of the best ways to make yourself feel better is to do things for other people, so making caramel apples may be a good thing.

After missing the tenth anniversary of the accident publication deadline, I set a new deadline for the ten-year class reunion for the class of 2005. That was another miss, but it's okay. I know I'm on God's time, and His timing is always perfect!

By January 1, 2016, the book still wasn't published, but we continued to try and help others. In April, Team Radio served lunch along with caring and encouragement to the families currently staying at "our Ronald McDonald House." I was so blessed to be able to give back to this organization that helped my family in its time of great need. The second annual "Play fore Eric" golf tournament was scheduled for August, and I was continuing to support the Ronald McDonald House.

June 5, 2016. I became an uncle again, as Erin and Kyle had their third baby, a baby boy named Chapman David Moore. Being an uncle has been one of the greatest blessings in my life. In addition, my parents celebrated their thirty-seventh anniversary on June 8. I am so thankful for them and their support, both before the accident and after.

June 12, 2016. Another anniversary of my accident date, this time the thirteenth. In addition, my uncle John passed away this day. He was only diagnosed with cancer three weeks prior. This was another reminder that life is short, so we have to make the most of the time we have. My life has been blessed with a wonderful family and great friends. My prayer for you is that you are as blessed as I have been. It is also my prayer that my life can be an example of the most important lesson I have ever learned, that no matter the circumstances and how bad a situation may look, that in all that can happen in the world, "Prayers work!"

August 5, 2016. Team Radio hosted the second annual "Play fore Eric" golf tournament to raise money for my foundation. This has become my favorite event because it is more than a golf tournament. In many ways, it turns into a reunion of old friends that I don't get to see as often as I would like. It also helps raise money for charities that I feel are important. This time I gave $4,000 for the new Commerce Boys and Girls Club. It opened a new facility in Commerce, and I wanted to help them as much as I could, too. In June we served lunch and took my wet slide and slip-n-slide for the kids to play on. We planned for that to be an annual event.

November 8, 2016. I got to do something today that a lot of people take for granted. Today I voted for the next president of the United States. Before she died, my Aunt Brenda said that Donald Trump would be the next president, and so I voted for him. I like that he is an outsider and isn't tied to political groups, and I hope that he will do what he is promising: "Make America great again!" I also hope that he will help small businessmen like me.

November 27, 2016. Team Radio made the trip to Atlanta to the Ronald McDonald House to serve dinner to the residents. It really doesn't seem that long ago that my family had to use the Ronald McDonald House, and I was so glad I was able to help these families in their time of trouble. My team of volunteers were really just good friends who jumped in whenever I wanted to do something, and I was blessed to have them. Doing this helped to take my mind off of the fact that Clemson beat my Gamecocks in football last weekend, too. It looked like Clemson might get to play for a national champion-ship again this year, which would make my sister happy, but I was ready for South Carolina to make it.

December 22, 2016. Today I did one of my favorite things to do—I sent a check for $6,000 to the Ronald McDonald House in Atlanta. There is no other charity I love more than this one, and I am glad that the "Play fore Eric" golf tournament was successful enough to be able to do this. I was also glad to have so many friends that helped me put together the tournament each year because, without them, it wouldn't happen. Now, I could enjoy Christmas with my family and friends.

January 9, 2017. Clemson beat Alabama to win the national championship. Erin was happy. To quote Forrest Gump, "That's all I have to say about that."

January 20, 2017. Today was a special day. For one thing, I turned thirty years old. The funny thing was I didn't feel that old. For another, President Trump was inaugurated today, so I spent my birthday watching the inauguration all day. Then, in a couple of days, my family and Hank Tiller and his family would be flying to Las Vegas to celebrate our birthdays, and I couldn't wait.

January 27, 2017. We arrived in Las Vegas for a couple of days. My parents, Erin and Kyle, and Uncle Tommy came as well as my best friend Hank with his wife and parents. David and Tabitha Evans also came, and I was glad because we had been friends since kindergarten as well. This was going to be a fun time and the best birthday I had had.

February 2, 2017. We were only home for a couple of days before we launched the next Team Radio fundraising project. We decided to sell chocolate-dipped strawberries by the dozen and half dozen for Valentine's Day. This year we were able to raise over $1,200, which was double from what we did last year. I was glad we improved this year, and hopefully we would do even more next year.

February 7, 2017. I had my checkup appointment at Shepherd's, and I had gained five pounds, which was good. Everything else was checking out good, too, and my memory was improving every day. God is good, and prayers work!

March 2017. Most people don't know this, but March is Traumatic Brain Injury Month. I like to spend most of the month sharing information about this issue. A lot of people suffer from TBI and don't even know it. For example, a concussion is a traumatic brain injury and can cause permanent damage. I am able to use social media to get information out and educate people. I just want everyone to know the effects of brain injuries and how they can impact their life. According to the Brain Injury Association of America TBI Fact Sheet, at least 3.5 million people have brain injuries every year; 2.5 million Americans have traumatic brain injuries, and 2.2 million have to be treated in emergency rooms. Their statistics show that someone has a brain injury every thirteen seconds. Tragically, an average of 137 people die every day due to a brain injury. Of those, 40.5 percent are from falls. I am in the 14.3 percent that are involved in auto accidents. For more information about brain injuries, go to www.biausa.org.[1]

April 29, 2017. Wow. It is still hard to believe what happened today. My friend, Karen Handel, was in a runoff election for Congress and President Trump came to speak at a rally for her. She emailed me a couple of days ago and invited me to come see him. After getting through all of the security checks, we went into a room set up for the president to speak—and we were in the front row on the left side! When he asked if anyone had questions, I raised my hand. He actually pointed at me, and I asked him how he felt about stem-cell research. Then he asked me why I was curious about that, so I told him that I was a traumatic brain injury survivor and I believed that this research could help me and others like me. He smiled at me and told me that he believed in the research and that he "was going to take care of me." I don't know what that means, but I can't believe that I was actually able to ask a question to the president of the

---

[1] *Brain Injury Facts and Statistics* (Vienna, VA: Brain Injury Association of America).

United States. Then he gave me a thumbs-up sign and asked the audience, "Doesn't he look great?" Coincidentally, I have always used the thumbs-up sign to let people know that I was okay, so I gave one back to the president.

May 2017. We were coming up on the fourteenth anniversary of my accident, and we were almost five years behind the publication date I had originally set. But when I looked back over those five years, I realized a lot had happened that I would have wanted to include in the book, so it just proved that God's timing is always best. We were having the third annual "Play fore Eric" golf tournament on August 5, and I was looking forward to it. This had begun as an effort to help me when I was in the hospital, and the same good ole friends who had started it fourteen years ago now helped me use it to raise money. Brit Jones, a local singer, was going to entertain the golfers during the dinner again this year. Team Radio will continue to have fundraising projects throughout the year to help various charities, as will a portion of the proceeds from this book. With the help of good friend and former bank executive Sandra Haggard, we are converting Team Radio into the Eric Redmon Foundation this year to supervise our fundraising efforts.

June 20, 2017. I am so happy tonight because my good friend Karen Handel was elected to Congress. Even though I don't live in her district, I had been supporting her and I thought she would do a good job. I sent her a text earlier today, and she texted me back most of the day. I don't know many candidates who would take the time to do that on election day. All I knew was that she had always been good to me and I was really happy for her. I was also happy for me, because one of the candidates I supported finally won! Plus, not only had I met and talked to the president of the United States, now I could talk to a congresswoman about the issues, too.

Although my accident has taken some things from me, it has given me much more. I have met so many wonderful people that I wouldn't have met otherwise. Most importantly, though, through the accident I have found my purpose—to help others. I like to think that I would have wanted to help others even without the accident, but I don't think I would be as passionate about it. It is my prayer that you find happiness and hope in my story. When I think about all I have been through, the two things that always come to mind are "Life's a party" and "Prayers work!" God bless and keep you.

***

The following thoughts are from some members of Team Radio:

MITCH REDMON: After graduation, I wondered what Radio would do. Now I look at the businesses he runs, the role model he has become, and I am amazed. Whenever someone is hurting, Radio is usually the first to try to help. He has had a bigger impact on people than anyone in our class. He has become a symbol of Commerce.

***

ANGIE REDMON: I am so proud of Eric and thankful for being able to go on this journey with him. He has changed, but much of the Radio we loved before the accident is still here. He has the same sense of humor and still loves everyone, but now he is very focused on what God wants him to do. Where I used to push him, now he drives himself to do things. I am happy to stop pushing him and merely to be his assistant with Life's A Party.

***

DAVID "ATT" STEPHENSON: As I said earlier, at first I did not think Eric was going to make it (survive). But I now know God had plans to use him. I have heard Eric give his testimony several times. He has spoken to my Fellowship of Christian Athletes group at school and to my youth group at church. His testimony is powerful. Eric is an inspiration to me and to a lot of others. He is one of the toughest competitors I have ever known. He gets that from his family.

***

KEVIN POE, certified physical therapist assistant: I never thought Eric's rehabilitation would take this long, and I know I gave the Redmons some false hopes at first by saying that we could do this. Of all the patients I have ever worked with, he had one of the worst brain injuries. Working with him now, I find it amazing to realize how much progress he has made. He can walk very well with a walker and with a cane if he's on good terrain. His attitude is unbelievable. I asked him if he has ever accepted that this may be as good as he will ever get. He told me that he would never accept that and would continue working as long as it takes. God has brought him this far, so who knows how far He will take him? I know that God is using Eric to inspire others because he has inspired me.

***

GREG JARVIS: My favorite thing about Radio is how he always wants to help people. For example, even though his mom has a tag that allows them to park in handicap parking spots, he refuses to use it. He tells his mom that someone else may need that spot more than he does. She lets him out at the door of a store and then parks in a regular spot. That's Radio—still refusing to accept that he is handicapped and always thinking about others. There have been many times that I have been inspired by his attitude and outlook on life. Words can't really explain what Radio means to me; all I can say is that knowing him has made me a better person.

***

TAFFY CARRUTH: All I can say is "Thank you, God, for letting me be in the right place at the right time." The Redmon family will forever hold a special place in my heart.

***

HANK TILLER: Radio is the best friend I could ever have and the toughest person I know.

***

JESSE SMITH: Radio has touched more lives than anyone I have ever met. The good Lord proved Radio is really strong, and Bobby and Miss Angie, too.

ACKNOWLEDGMENTS

There are so many people I want to thank for their part in my story. First, I have to thank God for sending His Son to be my Lord and Savior. Without Him, my story doesn't really matter. He has guided us throughout this effort and all the glory for our successes goes to Him.

Going back to June 12, 2003, I thank my "angel," Taffy Carruth, who noticed my accident and called for help. Next, many thanks to the Commerce EMTs and fire department, who stabilized me, carried me out of the woods, put me into an ambulance, loaded me onto a helicopter, and then drove Dad to Grady. I also thank the flight team and paramedics on the helicopter as well as the medical teams at Grady Memorial Hospital, as it was their skills and dedication that saved my life.

From my time in therapy, my eternal gratitude goes to Kevin Poe from Commerce, who has been working with me ever since the accident, and to Dr. Johnston and all the therapists and staff at Scottish Rite Hospital. I also appreciate the Ronald McDonald House staff and volunteers for providing a home away from home for us. Finally, to all my doctors, physical therapists, occupational therapists, and speech therapists in Atlanta, Athens, and Commerce: thank you for your skills and patience in working with me while my brain and body were healing and I was relearning how to do everything.

To my sports mentors—my cousins Michael and Gary Brown—and my coaches—Joe Hames, Steve Savage, and Att Stephenson—thank you for teaching me at an early age what it means to be a Commerce Tiger and that Commerce Tigers NEVER GIVE UP! To my teammates in all sports over the years, and especially my Thursday Night Crew, thank you for never letting me forget that I will always be a Commerce Tiger and you will always back me up.

To my extended family and church family who have helped Mom, Dad, Erin, and me for so many years, a huge thank-you. You are a big, loving family who was always with us before the accident, through our time at Grady and rehab, and even now. Special thanks go to the administration and staff of Commerce High School, especially Wes Massey, the aide who helped me daily, and to the administration of Commerce City Schools, in particular Dr. Susan Galis-White, who believed in me even without knowing me very well in the beginning. Heartfelt appreciation goes to Coach Greg Jarvis for believing in me as a coach, teacher, and friend, and for spending over thirteen years and countless long hours helping me put my story into words.

To my friends, well, there is no way I can individually thank all of you. My biggest problems are (1) there are so many of you, using all your names could triple the book's length; (2) with my memory issues and the passage of time, I worry about hurting feelings, leaving folks out, misattributing things, etc. and then having my editors compound those sins. That said, if your name isn't in the book, God and I know who you are and what you did. Whether you tutored me, helped me carry my books, or just welcomed me back to the community of Commerce, the high school, church, etc., I appreciate you more than I can ever express, and I ask God to bless you always.

To Mom and Dad, my rock in every calm or stormy sea before and after the accident, my heart overflows with love and appreciation. You have never given up on me, nor have you ever kept me from pushing forward, even when you had to do the pushing. You continue to entertain my friends, look for new research that can help me, and constantly seek to improve my quality of life. God couldn't have given me any greater parents than you are. Mom, you gave up your job in order to put me first, spent untold miserable hours with me in hospitals, clinics, and rehabilitation facilities, and continue to help me 24/7 with the challenges I face. Dad, you stayed up with me countless nights, built a physical therapy room and much of its equipment in our garage, learned to help me with my exercises even when doing them hurt you worse than me, and never allowed me to give up on myself when I got discouraged. Your parenting is tough love in action.

To my sister, Erin Redmon Moore, and her husband, Kyle Moore, who were and are always there for me. Erin, you gave up cheerleading at Clemson for a whole year, rearranged your academic schedule to help me with therapy and schoolwork, and tolerated my anger when aggravation seemed the only way to motivate me. You have been and always will be my best friend! Kyle, you have become the older brother I never had and have helped me whenever and however I've needed you. Thank you both for helping me and being there all along the way to support, encourage, and believe in me. Mostly, thank you for Cooper, Harper, and Chapman, who call me Ya Ya.

Of course, I want to thank my staff at Life's A Party. Our relationship is newer than the others, but you are the world's best workers and friends. I appreciate all your help to keep me and my company going and thriving.

"Miss Virginia" Meldrum, you took my manuscript and made it a story. Thank you for your long nights and many meetings around the dinner table. And for all the new friends I have made along this sometimes rocky way, I'm thankful that God opened doors to allow us to share our experiences. May God bless and keep you all.

Finally, to the City of Commerce and the surrounding area, there isn't enough room in the library for me to list everyone and every group who has helped us. Nor are there enough words in the dictionary to express my gratitude, but please know that I love you and thank God for Commerce, Georgia, and its people. No other place could have done a better job helping our family get through these challenging years.

'PPRECIATE IT!

ATTITUDE—DO YOU HAVE WHAT IT TAKES?

Greetings from Commerce, Georgia! I'm delighted to have this opportunity to share with you the lessons I've learned about the importance of attitude. These aren't book lessons and they didn't come easy. They were taught on football fields, golf courses, wrestling mats, hospital beds, and therapy tables.

I believe that attitude determines everything. It's a point of view about a set of circumstances, a way of talking and behaving that affects every aspect of your life. It's helpful to think of attitude as having three components: (1) what you think, (2) what you do, and (3) what you feel. My life experiences have caused my perspectives to grow and change over the years, and I'd like to tell you how my outlook on attitude developed.

In the early summer of 2003, I was a sixteen-year-old who loved his life and almost everyone in it. Like many teenagers, I played several sports, including football, golf, and wrestling. I had a great job, a wonderful girlfriend, a lot of friends, a decent academic average, and a nickname. Everyone in my small town called me "Radio" because I love to talk and don't have an off switch.

However, on June 12, 2003, I became known as a fighter, and Commerce became my support team. A horrible car accident on that summer evening changed my life forever with a traumatic brain injury, an unlikely rescue, a medevac flight, and a coma. Although they kept a positive attitude themselves, my parents said the doctors didn't know if I would make it or not.

Nothing could prepare me or my family for what lay ahead. In the blink of an eye, the life we had known was gone and we had to adjust to a new one. That spring I had been on a high-protein diet, working out really hard in the weight room and running every night to get in top shape. I thought I was getting my body in shape for the upcoming sports seasons; however, God was really getting me in shape for the biggest fight of my life—the fight for my life! Waking from my coma, I faced many challenges on the road to recovery. My biggest challenges were rebuilding short-term memory, speech, and enough control of my body to function on my own.

At first I couldn't remember anything from minute to minute. And in that situation, I learned to use many resources to help myself overcome my memory problems. Nobody wants to invite two girls over at the same time because he can't remember inviting the first one! To this day, my Blackberry is my best asset for battling memory challenges. The calendar in my phone helps me keep track of what I do each day and what I need to do. I never thought I'd be so dependent on electronic devices to help me through each day, but I've adjusted. The brain injury also left me unable to speak for the first three months after my accident. Radio without sound was a very frustrated Radio! With therapy, I learned to speak for a few seconds and then for minutes. My speech has improved considerably and continues to get stronger each day.

Walking is my biggest challenge. Muscle spasms make it hard for my legs to work normally. I didn't have a spinal injury, but my brain acts like a jittery quarterback. It sends extra-strong signals down the nervous system and causes my muscles to get very tight. My doctor told my family that my brain injury causes the spasms. In the beginning, my therapists stretched me every day and resorted to Botox and casts. All of this helped a little, but progress was very slow—and Botox didn't make me beautiful! It wasn't until I came home after two months at Scottish Rite and Dad added "redneck therapy" to my program that I began to show real improvement. I've continued to work hard through good times and rough times to get to where I am today, to regain the abilities I used to take for granted. Every day is a challenge now, but as I continue to work toward full recovery, my attitude continues to grow with me. That's how I make it through each day.

Life after the accident has taught me that attitude is a way of life. We have a choice every day regarding the attitude we embrace for that day. As they say, "The only difference between a good day and a bad day is your attitude." There are some things we can't change: our past, the way certain people feel about us or act toward us, or what's inevitable. We can't fix the crisis facing our economy or our political problems. Attitude is the only thing we can possibly change to deal with these situations more effectively. And in changing our attitudes, we can better control our own successes and failures because attitude determines outcome. This truth is accepted by most of the world's successful people whether they are doctors going into surgery, businessmen launching new ventures, or athletes playing tough opponents. This is true too for patients facing a discouraging diagnosis. Their attitudes provide the winning edge. A correct and willful attitude is the key to success.

I keep a card in my wallet with this quote from Charles Swindoll, a well-known Christian pastor, author, and educator: "The longer I live, the more I realize the impact of attitude on life." Do you realize the importance of this concept? In a nutshell, attitude is more important than education, money, circumstances, failures, successes, reality, or the past. Aside from my faith in Jesus Christ, my attitude is my best tool for a full recovery.

I am strongly convinced that life is only 10 percent what happens to me and 90 percent how I react to it. I may have been dealt a bad hand at the age of sixteen, but that's not going to stop me from achieving my goals and making the best of this life. After starting two successful businesses, I'm now considering starting a nonprofit organization to help those affected by car accidents and other traumatic events. As Mom says, "Prayer works!" Maintaining a positive attitude and my faith in God have helped me achieve success in spite of my circumstances. I'm living proof that attitude influences success. Because of my attitude, I have what it takes!

So think about this: do you have what it takes to succeed in your personal life no matter what your circumstances are? If not, can you change your attitude to work in your favor? This requires just three things: (1) change your thinking, (2) change the way you act, and (3) the hardest of all, change the way you feel. Since a positive attitude can open doors you may not know exist, reconsider your attitude today and move on to success!

God bless you all! Thank you, and remember, "Prayers work!"

About the Authors

 Eric Redmon was born in 1987 and was raised in Commerce, Georgia. He graduated from Commerce High School in the spring of 2005 after suffering a car accident in 2003. He is the founder and owner of Life's A Party, a party rental company, and was selected as the Kiwanian of the Year by the Commerce Kiwanis Club in 2016. Eric continues to live in his beloved Commerce with his parents.

Greg Jarvis, known simply as "Jarvis" in Commerce, began his teaching career at Commerce High School in 1993. He was selected STAR Teacher in 1999 and 2001 and Teacher of the Year for 2003–2004. In 2004, he moved to Mill Creek High School and was selected its Teacher of the Year in for 2015–2016. In 2017, the senior class selected him for the Lasting Impression Award. He continues to live in Commerce with his wife, Lauren, and three children, Jaxson, Jaycie, and Charlee Faith.

CONNECT WITH ERIC

Website: www.ericredmonfoundation.com

FB: ericredmonfoundation

Twitter: @ericlredmon

Instagram: ericredmonfoundation